MASSEY FERGUSON 35 TRACTOR

The Workshop Service Manual

ALSO COVERS FERGUSON TO35 MODELS

MASSEY FERGUSON 35 TRACTOR

The Workshop Service Manual

ALSO COVERS FERGUSON TO35 MODELS

Chris Jaworski

Old Pond
PUBLISHING

The Massey Ferguson 35 Tractor

Old Pond Publishing is an imprint of Fox Chapel Publishers International Ltd.

Project Team
Editor: Sarah Bloxham
Layout: Liz Whatling

ISBN 978-1-912158-51-5

A catalogue record for this book is available from the British Library.

Fox Chapel Publishers International Ltd.
20-22 Wenlock Rd.
London N1 7GU, U.K.

Fox Chapel Publishing
903 Square Street
Mount Joy, PA 17552, U.S.A

www.oldpond.com

Printed and bound in China
Second Printing

Acknowledgements

My grateful thanks to the following for their help and support:
Bicton College engineering staff and students, George French,
Nick Jackman, Ray Pile, Raymond Taylor, Vapormatic Ltd
and Bill Vellacott, and of course, my wife Pam.
To my special grandchildren Ben, Evelyn, Hugo and Livvy.

Contents

Safety   6

Introduction   7

1 **Buying and Safety**   11

2 **Weekly Checks**   20

3 **Operator Maintenance**   23

4 **Engines**   31
- 4-cylinder 23c diesel engine
  overhaul 33
- 4-cylinder 87mm Petrol/TVO
  engine overhaul 51
- 3-cylinder 3.152 engine overhaul 68

5 **Cooling Systems**   80

6 **Fuel Systems**   87
- Carburettors 87
- Fuel lift pump overhaul 93
- 3-cylinder diesel fuel system 95
- 4-cylinder diesel fuel system 99
- Air cleaner operation
  and service 103
- Diesel fuel injectors 105
- DPA type distributor
  fuel injection pump 109

7 **Transmissions**   112
- 3-cylinder engine clutch repair 112
- 4-cylinder engine double clutch
  and flywheel overhaul 118
- Single clutch and flywheel
  overhaul 121
- Six-speed gearbox overhaul 124
- Multi-power gearbox overhaul 131

8 **Rear Axle and PTO**   138

9 **Brakes**   144

10 **Hydraulic System**   150

11 **Steering and Front Axle**   156

12 **Electrics**   162
- Disposal of a lead acid battery 162
- Inertia starter test and repair 164
- Pre-engaged starter system
  test and repair 169
- 3-cylinder electrics 174
- 4-cylinder electrics 179
- Petrol/TVO electrics 182

13 **Bodywork**   187
- Bonnet repair 187
- Paintwork 194
- Fitting a new bonnet 200

Safety

Before carrying out any maintenance on your tractor it is important to remember a few safety rules:

- Use lots of trays/containers for the disassembled parts and use masking tape to label them where required.

- Always use axle stands with hydraulic jacks.

- Beware of sharp casing – machine-edge cuts are easily made when lifting.

- When setting up for a job be sure to choose level ground to work on.

- Wear protective gloves when working with oils/fluids.

- Be careful when dismantling the major components as it can affect the stability of the chassis unit.

- Beware of moving parts if making adjustments to them.

- Work slowly and carefully. Haste is a common cause of accidents.

- All fluids and filters have to be disposed of responsibly either at a recycling point or by a local dealer. They cannot be deposited in domestic waste.

- Use masking or duct tape to block off any open fuel lines to prevent dirt from entering.

- Battery acid is highly corrosive. It is advisable to wear goggles and protective gloves when working with the battery.

- Be careful when working with hot engine oil.

- Wear protective goggles when working with antifreeze.

- Be careful to avoid splashing oil or antifreeze on your clothes or skin.

- Only operate the ignition key from the driver's seat.

- Allow the engine to cool before draining coolant or replacing any parts.

- Ensure the engine is cold or allow it to cool for at least an hour before removing the radiator cap.

- Wear a dust mask when cleaning the paper air filter.

- Use oxy-acetylene with care and beware of potential fire hazards.

- Always replace axle sets, i.e. fit new shoes or lining to both the left-hand and right-hand brakes.

- Beware of asbestos brake dust.

- Dampen down dust with brake cleaner. Do not use airline to clean off dust.

- Wear gloves and a dust mask when removing and/or cleaning brakes.

- Care must be taken when removing brake return springs.

- Always disconnect the battery before working on the electrical system.

- Unsure of a task? Ask someone who is more experienced or consult a professional.

Disclaimer

All reasonable steps have been taken to ensure that the information in
The Massey Ferguson 35 Tractor Workshop Service Manual is correct.
Care should always been taken when performing the procedures outlined in this manual
and when in doubt please consult a professional. The author and publisher cannot
be held liable or responsible for any kind of injury or damage that may result to the
reader or a third party as a result of the use of this book.

The History of the Massey Ferguson 35

This workshop manual covers Massey Ferguson 35 tractors from 1956 to 1964. During this period, over 387,000 tractors were produced, making the MF 35 one of the most popular tractors produced. This manual will prove invaluable to the potential buyer, operator and restoration enthusiast because of its simple and logical approach to tackling even the most daunting of tasks. Each chapter is written concisely to enable the reader to carry out maintenance work and understand the components of the tractor. Within each chapter certain jobs are explained using a logical photographic sequence; these will help the reader to safely perform repairs or major restoration.

The Massey Ferguson 35 tractors were updated versions of the Ferguson TE 20 range with a number of new features, including an up-rated engine, a dual clutch option to provide live-drive PTO and a dual range gearbox to increase forward speeds from four to six or twelve with Multi-Power option. The MF 35s also had ground speed PTO and increased hydraulic lift capacity with separate draft and position controls.

Two versions were available: the standard and the De-Luxe. The latter version was fitted with the dual clutch, live PTO, differential lock, tractormeter, step assemblies and cushion foam seat as standard. But, as was commonly found, options could be retrofitted later.

Grey and Gold

The first of the Ferguson 35 tractors were built in October 1956 at the Banner Lane factory in Coventry, England. These were painted with grey tinwork and metallic copper-coloured castings. The tractors were officially called the FE35s but were often referred to simply as the 'grey and golds'. Power was provided from a Standard Motor Company petrol/TVO or 23c 4-cylinder diesel engine. Both engines were updated versions of the ones previously used in the TE 20s.

The Standard 23c diesel engine featured a larger bore, an improved rotary fuel injection pump and new cylinder head design which enabled it to produce 37 bhp.

Ferguson grey and gold Petrol/TVO model

A genuine original

The Petrol/TVO/lamp oil engines were similar to the TE 20 engines but bored out to 87 mm and fitted with a new carburettor. Their outputs increased to 37, 30 and 29 bhp respectively.

Transition to Massey Ferguson 35

Massey-Harris and Ferguson merged on 12 August 1953 and the new company was known as Massey-Harris-Ferguson. The company name was changed to Massey-Ferguson (note the hyphen) following an announcement on 19 November 1957, but then the hyphen was dropped early in 1958. The now familiar triple triangle logo also emerged as a part of global reorganisation.

The production colour changed from grey and gold (with the last tractor produced in this livery at serial number 74655) to the more familiar – and standard across the entire Massey Ferguson range – red bonnet, wings and grey castings in late 1957.

Bonnets, Wings and Castings

The two push button bonnet catches that first appeared on the FE 35 were used until 1959 (specifically serial number 141140) after which a swivel catch was fitted on top of the bonnet lid itself. The six-stud outer half shaft housing that was used on the grey and gold tractors continued to be used for the production of the first 2972 red and grey Massey Ferguson badged tractors before being replaced with the twelve-stud version on later castings.

There were many small changes and options to the tractors over the period of manufacture. The first of the Perkins engine tractors retained the old-style air inlet under the bonnet, but this changed to the raised 'mushroom' air cleaner intake that went through the bonnet and had to be removed before the bonnet could be lifted.

In 1962 the wings changed from the shell design to the extension mudguards that connected to revised footplates. This change was made to ensure health and safety compliance.

Engines and Transmission

In January 1959, Massey Ferguson acquired Perkins engines and took over the Banner Lane factory from Standard Motor Co. This move enabled them to adopt the Perkins A3.152 engine (from serial number 165596).

MF 35 23c 4-cylinder

MF 35 3-cylinder restored

In 1962, the MF 35 was improved with the addition of an optional differential lock and Power Adjusted Variable Track (PAVT) rear wheels. This enabled the rear track width to be altered by simply driving the tractor forwards or backwards at which point the wheels would 'wind' in or out.

In December 1962, a new gearbox was introduced called the 'Multi-Power'. This gearbox was able to achieve a higher gear through a power-operated wet clutch without de-clutching, thus giving twelve forward and four reverse gears and a slightly higher road speed.

MF 35X

The last change in 1962 came with the introduction of the Massey Ferguson 35X, which used an up-rated AD3.152 direct-injection engine and resulted in a power increase to 44.5 bhp.

MF 35X 3-cylinder 3.152

MF 135

The last MF 35 tractors were produced in 1964 before Massey Ferguson announced their new 'Red Giants'. This was the result of four years of development and produced the 100 series tractors. The MF 35 had undergone 598 changes in order to emerge as the MF 135 tractor.

MF 35X 3-cylinder Multi-Power

Chapter 1   Buying and Safety

Prior to potential purchase an assessment must be made in order to ascertain whether the tractor is priced correctly. This will be influenced by a number of factors including how much it will to cost to fully restore or to mechanically overhaul the tractor and whether or not you are willing to commit the time and effort to refurbish an 'old dog'. Once the tractor has been purchased a more detailed examination hopefully will not reveal any nasty (read expensive) surprises.

Three Essential Checks

There are three checks that you can perform upon viewing a potential purchase. The first two checks (see chart) can be made easily with a knowledgeable friend or local agricultural engineer. It is unwise for the inexperienced person to buy a tractor on looks alone as shiny paint can hide a multitude of problems. The third check requires technical tools and knowledge to complete effectively, but will usually only confirm the expert's opinion of the condition.

1   Tractor component visual condition

Tractor make	Massey Ferguson
Model	35
Registration number	123 ABC this should relate to the V5 document and the casting age marks
Engine condition	**Good** – Starts easily and quickly from cold; no strange noises; when revving engine some black smoke; pulls well when driven; no oil leaks; good oil pressure on dash gauge. **Average** – Starts with good battery; some blue/black smoke; slight oil stains. **Poor** – Difficult starting and needs a good battery and a sniff of ether spray to fire into life. Excessive crankcase compression (oil blowing out of the dip stick hole). Engine oil leaking from the front and rear oil seals. Low oil pressure indicated on the dash oil gauge. Rattle/knocking noises from internal engine.
Electrics	**Good** – New battery; terminals tight and in good condition; wiring insulation good and secured; charging light goes out upon starting and ancillary electrics (wipers, heater, lights, etc.) working . **Average** – Battery starts tractor but is more than two years old; wiring needs attention, securing and some repairs. Most ancillaries work. **Poor** – Very old battery requires jump start; no battery charging evident. Wiring condition frayed, unsecured and disconnected/ broken. Requires new loom. Starter motor operation poor when new battery fitted. Charging ammeter not working. Lighting and other ancillaries not working.
Transmission	CLUTCH **Good** – Gear selection and changing smooth and easy; no noises when clutch pedal depressed; free play correct; clutch stalls engine when clutch slip test carried out. **Average** – Clutch slight drag and sticking in gear possibly due to lack of use; PTO moves in and out of gear easily. Free play needs attention. **Poor** – Difficulty engaging and disengaging gears without grinding noise; judder when taking up drive; clutch will not stall engine on clutch slip test; noise from clutch housing when pedal depressed.

Transmission (continued)	GEARBOX/ REAR AXLE
	Good – No whine or bearing whine noise from gearbox; gear levers select range easily; 'change on the move' 'Multi-Power' range works efficiently.
	Average – Some low noise evident; gear levers lift up and down too much. Some side play inside selectors.
	Poor – Difficult to select gears; jumps out on over run; loud gear and bearing noise; 'change on the move' range not working.
Brakes	**Good** – Pedal has good feel/bite; brakes hold on hill and slow tractor when applied in a straight line; pedal free play correct; hand brake catch works well.
	Average – Pedal free play needs adjusting; effort needed to slow tractor; hand brake works on last catch. Adjustment required.
	Poor – Both clutch and brake pedal have lost diamond grip indicating hard life/work carried out. Oil leaks evident from rear axle seals onto brake drums; poor stopping ability; hand brake will not hold tractor on slope.
Steering	**Good** – Steering wheels react quickly with no play when steering wheel wobbled; no play in steering joints, no free play in wheel bearings and king pins; front axle pivot pin secure.
	Average – Slight play inside steering box (in straight ahead position) as well as in steering joints, wheel bearings and king pins.
	Poor – Excessively worn and slack in steering components; front wheel bearings noisy and loose; excessive play in the trunnion pin and bushes. Drag links bent both sides. Steering wheel disintegrating.
Hydraulics	**Good** – Rear linkage arms and top link have little play and adjustable arm moves freely; responds quickly to operating levers movement and will lift a heavy load (3-furrow plough). Test oil pressure: 175 bar (2,500 psi) is good.
	Average – Slight wear in rear linkage; lubrication and some adjustment required. Oil pressure slightly below maximum.
	Poor – Very worn pins and link arms; excessive play in top link draft spring housing; oil pressure well below maximum limit; rear arms will not lift heavy load, hydraulic pump noisy on full load.
Tyres	**Good** – Front and rear tyres new and same brand with no cuts or surface cracks; all hold air pressure. Rims in good condition: no damage and rusting, pitting.
	Average – 50% worn fronts and rears with slight perishing; different brands. Slight rim damage and light pitting to rims.
	Poor – Front and rear tyres 80% worn and cracking on surfaces with cuts on side walls. Both rims dented and very badly corroded.
Body work	**Good** – Unmolested as original with good paintwork and no damage due to corrosion or accidents to body work. No badges or lights missing. Well looked after with V5 registration log book present.
	Average – Some good repairs carried out over time; working order but may need tidying to reach a good condition; some cosmetic parts missing. V5 registration log book not present but registration number available.
	Poor – Very badly damaged and corroded body work in need of replacement or extensive repair; no badges or complete lighting. No V5 document or registration plate.

The above chart can act as a guide to help you determine:

(a) whether the tractor is really worth purchasing and/or haggling down the price;
(b) and the initial cost of the restoration, bearing in mind it will always cost more than anticipated.

2 Identifying the originality

This helps to understand the production codes, serial and model numbers and transmission code interpretation. Each major casting on the tractor has a casting manufacturing date embossed on its surface, e.g.:

Rear transmission casting number	K-16-L
Rear axle trumpet housings casting number	K-10-L
Bell housing casting number	J-3-L
Tractor serial number	SNMYW343872
Engine serial number	1997156C

Therefore our interpretation of the tractor age from the bell housing numbering:

J = Month = October, **K** = November, **L** = December.

3 = day of the month

L = Letters related to year of manufacture

The following table shows the serial numbers of the tractor and the corresponding year of manufacture letter prefix as found on the component castings:

MF 35		
Year	**Prefix**	**Tractor serial number**
1957	F	74656-79552
1958	G	79553-125067
1959	H	125068-171470
1960	I	171471-220613
1961	J	220614-267527
1962	K	267528-307230
1963	L	307231-352254
1964	M	352255-388382

The engine casting mark is K-16-L.

This gives us the date of manufacture as (K) November 16 (L) 1963 which coincides age-wise with all the other casting marks. This indicates the major casting components are highly likely to be the originals and the tractor has not had any major casting swaps. Changing of the castings often occurs when people are trying to achieve a cheap restoration. They will swap complete engines, gearboxes or rear axles instead of repairing the internal components. This action may detract from the originality of the finished tractor.

The tractor serial number **SNMYW343872** is explained as follows:

S = Normal width tractor

N = Diesel A3.152 engine

M = Dual clutch

Y = Differential lock

W = Multi-Power transmission

As all the options are fitted to the tractor we can safely assume it is a factory original.

Other serial number codes are as follows:

Chassis

S = Normal width tractor

V = Vineyard width tractor

J = Industrial tractor

C = High clearance tractor

Engine

G = Petrol engine (6:1)

H = Petrol high altitude (6.6:1)

D = Diesel standard 23C

K = Petrol/TVO standard

L = Lamp oil standard

N = Diesel A3.152 engine

B = Gas (butane) standard

Clutch

F = Single

M = Dual

Transmission

W = Multi-Power

Y = Differential lock

3 Technical assessment

Cylinder compression test

To ascertain the condition of an engine we can carry out a cylinder compression test. This involves removing the fuel injectors and replacing them with a dummy injector and pressure gauge. Typical results recorded are:

Cylinder number	**Dry test psi**	**Wet test psi**
1	300	330
2	200	210
3	250	310

The 'wet' test involves squirting 8–10 shots of engine oil into each cylinder using an oil can. This seals the piston rings and the compression readings will normally rise.

The above results show that the engine is worn and will not start easily (ideally it should be above 380 psi minimum) without utilising starting (ether) spray because of the low internal cylinder pressure reading. The piston rings are then sealed by adding the oil into each of the engine cylinders. If the readings increase by more than 25–30 psi, the rings and or bores are worn, i.e. not sealing. If the reading remains the same, the compression loss is due to a fault above the pistons, i.e. head gasket or leaking inlet/exhaust valves. The lower reading indicates that there is obviously a more serious problem with cylinder number 2.

Note: when carrying out the above test on a Massey Ferguson 35 petrol/TVO engine a pressure gauge is screwed into the spark plug hole (on the respective cylinder to be tested) and all the spark plugs must be removed to permit the engine to turn over quickly.

The readings for an engine in good condition are 90 to 100 psi, any lower than this and a 'wet' test should be carried out as per the diesel test to ascertain where the loss of compression has occurred.

Using a PTO-driven dynamometer can easily highlight the following faults:

- Engine power and torque output
- Engine breathing
- Clutch slip transmission and PTO
- Oil and fuel leaks
- Blocked air cleaner
- Cooling system operation

- Unusual noises or vibrations
- Exhaust smoke colour
  - Blue – worn engine
  - White – coolant leak into engine
  - Black – fuel system problem and misfire or air cleaner blocked

Rear hydraulic oil pressure test

A hydraulic oil pressure gauge can be connected to the tapping, supplying the trailer tipping pipe feed, and readings taken with the oil hot, i.e. after operating the tractor with the arms in the fully raised position for over one hour. A pressure reading of 172 bar (2,500 psi) is the tractor's specification. This indicates a good pump and/or pressure relief valve.

1.02. Genuine original

1.02. This is a rare example of a one farm from new tractor. It has been used but was well cared for with regular repairs and servicing to keep it in good condition. If the tractor came up for sale it would achieve top market price because of its originality. It would be unfortunate if it was re-painted as this tractor is invaluable to restorers to check for originality of parts.

1.01. Typical hedgerow

1.01. A typical hedgerow tractor probably would have been exposed to the elements for many years and therefore care must be taken in examining it to ascertain the extent of the harm done. The engine is likely to be stuck due to water ingress and the tyres perished because of ultra-violet light deterioration. Therefore repair costs must be realistically considered.

1.03. Fully restored

1.03. To save the problems, time and knowledge required to carry out a restoration one option is to buy a tractor that is already finished. Again this will require a high initial outlay on purchasing the tractor, but guarantees that the tractor will be ready to use. One downside is that one does not know the 'level' of the restoration. Was it just a paint job and a few replacement parts or a full, expensive rebuild? Photographs of the restoration would give the prospective buyer the necessary information.

1.04. Blow by

1.04. As the engine is revved and the engine oil becomes warm, it is seen to blow out of the dipstick hole. This fault indicates that there are compression gases leaking past the worn piston rings and bore and pressurising the crankcase (sump), thus forcing out the oil.

1.05. Blue exhaust

1.05. As the engine is revved, oil is drawn past the worn piston rings and bore and is burnt by the engine. This is indicated by the blue tint of the exhaust smoke.

1.06. Dynamometer test

1.06. The PTO-driven oil-operated dynamometer is connected the tractor PTO shaft via a torque transducer (the small black unit fitted to the tractor PTO). This unit measures the twist of the PTO shaft (torque) and the speed in RPM and then calculates accurately (+ or – 1%) the power available.

1.07. Rear axle serial number

1.07. To ensure the tractor casings, and therefore the internal parts, are from the original tractor that left the factory, the casting date numbers can be checked using the reference charts. The dates should all coincide with each other within a few months and the same year. The rear casing number is just in front of the round inspection cover on the left-hand side of the axle, i.e. K16L.

1.08. Multi-Power test

1.08. If the tractor is fitted with a Multi-Power change-on-the-move high/low gearbox, this must be checked for correct operation. Test 1 is carried out on an incline; the tractor is driven up the hill in high and then the clutch is depressed. As the tractor rolls backwards the transmission should 'lock up' and stop the tractor, thus confirming that the Multi-Power is ok. The second test involves driving the tractor at various speeds and on differing inclines to check that the Multi-Power lever selects and de-selects high and low firmly and positively. Drive for at least two miles or one hour to bring the engine and transmission to working temperature then carry out tests again.

1.09. Hydraulic pump test

1.09. Since the hydraulic arms raise and lower with the movement of the operating lever, we know that oil pressure is present. By connecting an oil pressure gauge to the tipping pipe outlet, we can confirm that our reading shows an operating pressure of 2,000 psi. This is below the recommended operating pressure of 2,500 psi, thus indicating a worn hydraulic pump or relief valve.

1.10. Check wear of link arms

1.10. Grab the two lower link arms and lift them, this will reveal any play in the pins and joints. As is typical of a yard tractor, the link arms flopped and rattled all over the place. New arms and pins will definitely be needed. Note the oil leaking from the lower arm pins under the trumpet housings; this indicates loose pins in the housing.

1.11. Play in draft spring

1.11. Hold the top draft spring attachment point and pull it in and out; there should be only a very small amount of free play. This tractor has lots and therefore the internal hydraulic linkage will need to be inspected and parts replaced.

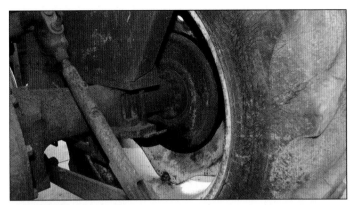

1.12. Oil leak onto brakes

1.12. The rear trumpet housings have oil seals in the ends of the half shaft housing. Unfortunately when they leak the oil reaches the brakes as shown by the oil stain. Replacing these seals is a major job and requires special tools and oxy-acetylene equipment.

1.13. Diesel compression testing

1.13. To determine the engine condition we can carry out a cylinder compression test. This involves removing the fuel injectors and replacing them with a dummy injector and pressure gauge.

1.14. Petrol compression test

1.14. When carrying out a compression test on a Massey Ferguson 35 with a petrol/TVO engine, a pressure gauge is screwed into the spark plug hole (on the respective cylinder to be tested). All the spark plugs must be removed to permit the engine to turn over quickly.

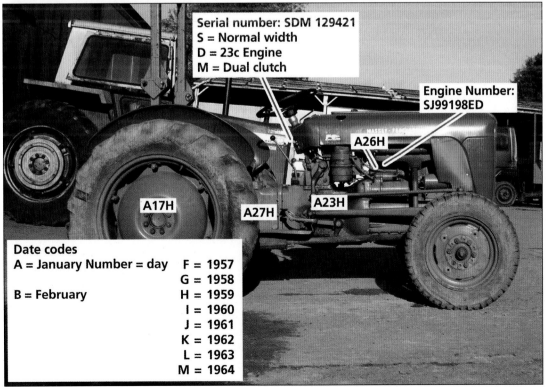

Serial number: SDM 129421
S = Normal width
D = 23c Engine
M = Dual clutch

Engine Number: SJ99198ED

A26H

A17H   A27H   A23H

Date codes
A = January Number = day   F = 1957
                            G = 1958
B = February   H = 1959
                            I = 1960
                            J = 1961
                            K = 1962
                            L = 1963
                            M = 1964

1.15. Date ageing

1.15. Number and letter marks in the major castings indicate the date of manufacture and therefore whether the major parts – e.g. engine, gearbox or rear axle centre castings – have been replaced in the tractor's life.

General Safety

Avoid fires

When you work around fuel, do not smoke or work near heaters or other fire hazards. Make sure to store flammable fluids away from fire hazards. Do not incinerate or puncture pressurised containers. Make sure the machine that you are using is clean of rubbish, grease and debris. Do not store oily rags; they can ignite and burn spontaneously.

Cooling system

An explosive release of fluids from a pressurised cooling system could cause serious burns. Shut off the engine. Only remove the filler cap when cool enough to touch with bare hands. Slowly loosen cap to first stop to relieve pressure before removing completely.

Prepare for emergencies

- Be prepared if a fire starts.
- Keep a first aid kit and fire extinguisher handy.
- Keep a record of emergency numbers for doctors, ambulance, fire service and hospital.
- Attend a first aid course.

Battery safety

A few useful tips about battery safety:

- Caution: battery gas (hydrogen) can explode. Keep sparks and naked flames away from batteries.
- Use a torch to check battery electrolyte level.
- Never check battery charge by placing a metal object (i.e. a spanner) across the posts. Use a voltmeter or hydrometer.
- Always remove grounded (earth) battery clamp first and replace it last.
- Caution: sulphuric acid in battery electrolyte is poisonous. It is strong enough to burn skin, burn holes in clothing, and cause blindness if splashed into eyes.

Avoid the hazards by:

1. Filling batteries in a well-ventilated area.
2. Wearing eye protection and rubber gloves.
3. Avoiding breathing fumes when electrolyte is added.
4. Avoiding spilling or dripping electrolyte.
5. Using proper jump-start procedure.

If you spill acid on yourself, take the following precautions:

1. Flush your skin with water.
2. Apply baking soda to help neutralise the acid.
3. Flush your eyes with water for 15–30 minutes. Get medical attention immediately.

If acid is swallowed:

1. Do not induce vomiting.
2. Drink large amounts of water or milk, but do not exceed two litres.
3. Get medical attention immediately.

Warning: Battery posts, terminals and related accessories contain lead and lead compounds and chemicals; therefore, wash hands after handling or wear protective gloves.

High-pressure fluids

Escaping fluid under pressure can penetrate the skin causing serious injury. Avoid the hazard by relieving pressure before disconnecting hydraulic or fuel lines. Tighten all connections before applying pressure. Search for leaks with a piece of cardboard. Protect hands and body from high-pressure fluids. If an accident occurs, see a doctor immediately. Any fluid injected into the skin must be surgically removed.

Wear protective clothing

- Wear close-fitting clothing and safety equipment appropriate to the job. Strong boots or steel toe-capped boots are preferable.
- Prolonged exposure to loud noise can cause impairment or loss of hearing. Wear a suitable hearing protection device such as earmuffs or earplugs to protect against objectionable or uncomfortable loud noises.
- Operating equipment safely requires the full attention of the operator. Do not wear radio or music headphones while operating machinery.

Machine safety

Tie long hair behind your head. Do not wear a necktie, scarf, loose clothing or necklace when you work near machine tools or moving parts. If these items were to get caught, severe injury could result. Remove rings, watches and other jewellery to prevent electrical shorts and entanglement in moving parts.

Work in a ventilated area

Engine exhaust fumes can cause sickness or death. If it is necessary to run an engine in an enclosed area, remove the exhaust fumes from the area with an exhaust pipe extension. If you do not have an exhaust pipe extension, open the doors and get outside air into the area.

Work in clean area

Before starting a job:

- Clean work area and machine.
- Make sure you have all necessary tools and parts for the job.
- Read all instructions thoroughly; do not attempt shortcuts.

Remove paint before welding or heating

- Avoid potentially toxic fumes and dust. Hazardous fumes can be generated when paint is heated by welding, soldering or by using a gas torch.
- Do all work outside or inside a well-ventilated area and properly dispose of paints and solvents.
- Make sure to remove paint before welding or heating. If you sand or grind paint, avoid breathing in the dust by wearing an approved respirator.
- If you use solvent or paint stripper, remove stripper with soap and water before welding. Remove solvent or paint stripper containers and other flammable material from the intended work area. Allow fumes to disperse for at least 20 minutes before welding or heating.

Avoid heating near pressurised fluid lines

Flammable spray can be generated by heating near pressurised fluid lines, resulting in severe burns to yourself and bystanders. Do not heat by welding, soldering, or using a gas torch near pressurised fluid lines or other flammable materials. Pressurised lines can be accidentally cut when heat goes beyond the immediate flame area.

Illuminate work area safely

Illuminate your work area adequately but safely. Use a portable safety light for working inside or under the machine. LED torches produce a safe level of illumination with long life.

Lifting equipment

Lifting heavy components incorrectly can cause severe injury or machine damage. Make sure to follow the recommended procedure for removal and installation of components. Use specific lifting chains or straps and not home-made ones.

Construct dealer-made tools safely

Faulty or broken tools can result in serious injury. When constructing tools, use proper, quality materials and good workmanship. Do not weld tools unless you have the proper equipment and experience to perform the job.

Practise safe maintenance

- Keep your area clean. It is also important that it is dry.
- Understand the service procedure before doing the work.
- Never lubricate, service, or adjust a machine while it is moving. Keep hands, feet and clothing from power-driven parts. Disengage all power and operate controls to relieve pressure. Lower the equipment to the ground. Stop the engine. Remove the key. Allow the machine to cool.
- Securely support axle stands and any machine elements that must be raised for service work.
- Keep all parts in good condition and properly installed. Fix damage immediately.
- Replace worn or broken parts.
- Install all guards and shields after any repairs.
- Remove any build-up of grease, oil, or debris.
- On tractors, disconnect battery ground cable (earth) before making adjustments on electrical systems or welding on the machine.

Use proper tools

- Use tools appropriate to the work. Makeshift tools and procedures can create safety hazards.
- Use power tools only to loosen threaded parts and fasteners.
- For loosening and tightening nuts and bolts, use the correct size tools to avoid injury caused by slipping.

Properly dispose of waste

- Improperly disposing of waste can threaten the environment. Potentially harmful waste used with equipment includes oil, fuel, coolant, brake fluid, filters and batteries.
- Use leak-proof containers when draining fluids. Do not use food or drink containers that may mislead someone into drinking from them.
- Do not pour waste onto the ground, down a drain or into any water source. Contact local environment agency or recycling centre for advice on the proper way to recycle or dispose of waste.

Chapter 2 Weekly Checks

Whether you are rushing around to shows, road runs, ploughing matches or just simply using your tractor for trailer or three-point-linkage work it is advisable to carry out basic checks on the tractor each time it is used. This routine will not only maintain the reliability of the tractor but also provide time to note problems early, which can save expense or further damage.

These 'weekly checks' can be carried out in a short amount of time. The under-bonnet checks will vary slightly because of the three engine options fitted to the Massey Ferguson 35 tractor, but the gearbox, rear axle, steering, hydraulics and brakes are all virtually the same.

The fuel sediment bowl is usually of glass construction so any sediment and water will be visible at the bottom of the bowl. If necessary, remove the bowl and wash out.

When checking the engine coolant level, ensure the engine is cold otherwise scalding hot coolant will blow out of the radiator when the cap is removed. The level should be just below the lip on the radiator. If topping up, use a 50% mixture of antifreeze and water to maintain frost protection (-34 °Celsius). Never use just water as this will dilute the antifreeze.

If you are using the tractor on the road then visibility for you and other road users is important, so check that all the lights and wipers (if fitted) are working efficiently and that screens are clean and grease free.

Keep the diesel tank filled to the brim to prevent condensation building up inside. Ideally, petrol fuel tanks should not be kept too full as the petrol will evaporate quickly. If the tractor is not going to be used for longer than a week running the tractor until the engine stops helps to prevent the possibility of leaving a gummy petrol substance behind which can block the carburettor jets. This will remove any petrol residue from the carburettor.

Tools required for checks:

Range of metric/imperial spanners and socket sets

Flat blade screwdrivers

Battery hydrometer

Copper grease

Grease gun

Antifreeze tester

Torque wrench

Dust masks

Protective gloves

Note: if using a Petrol/TVO engine tractor always switch over from TVO to petrol a few minutes before stopping the engine as the engine will not restart with TVO fuel in the carburettor.

2.01. Leaks

2.01. Check the tractor for signs of fluid leaks daily. The abbreviations give the type of leak expected for each area on the tractor. (MF 35 3-cylinder diesel version shown.)

FO	Fuel oil leak
CO	Coolant leak
EO	Engine oil leak
TO	Transmission oil leak
SO	Steering oil leak

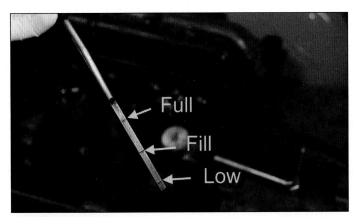

2.02. Dipstick marks

2.02. To check the amount of oil in the engine sump make sure the tractor is on level ground, then remove the dipstick from the engine ensuring the tractor engine has been stopped for at least 20 minutes. The oil level mark should always be maintained between the middle and up to 'full' line on the dipstick. Do not operate the tractor with the oil at the low mark as this could cause engine damage.

2.03. Air cleaner

2.03. After removing the clamp, the lower bowl can be removed and the oil inspected. Wash out and clean, then refill with 1 pint (0.57 litres) of clean engine oil to maximum mark only. If the bowl is overfilled the engine could draw the oil into the

combustion and will over-rev, which could seriously damage it. The intervals for cleaning depend on the conditions in which the tractor is working. It may need cleaning several times a day in very dusty conditions. Warning signs to look out for are loss of power and black exhaust smoke.

2.04. Checking tyre pressures

2.04. To maintain traction in fieldwork and low wear rates on the road the tyre pressures should be checked regularly and adjusted accordingly. Using an accurate pressure gauge, check and adjust tyre pressures to 1.8 bar (26 psi) front and 0.83 bar (12 psi) rear; if using a front loader increase front pressure to 2.07 bar (30 psi).

2.05. 3-cylinder Diesel AD.3.152 engine – left-hand view

2.06. 3-cylinder Diesel AD.3.152 engine – right-hand view

2.07. 4-cylinder Petrol/TVO engine – left-hand view

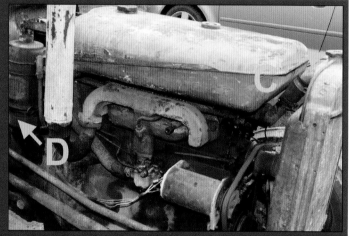

2.08. 4-cylinder Petrol/TVO engine – right-hand view

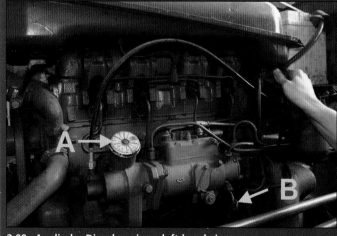

2.09. 4-cylinder Diesel engine – left-hand view

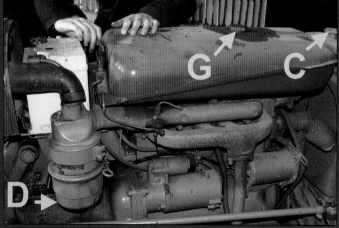

2.10. 4-cylinder Diesel engine – right-hand view

Labels of weekly check points.		
A Engine oil filler cap	**E** Petrol fuel tank	
B Engine oil dipstick	**F** TVO fuel tank	
C Engine coolant (radiator cap)	**G** Diesel fuel tank	
D Air cleaner oil bath type	**H** Fuel sediment bowl	

Chapter 3 Operator Maintenance

This chapter is designed to assist the enthusiast in maintaining their Massey Ferguson tractor for safety, reliability and longevity. The information on weekly checks and general layout of the engine is covered in Chapter 2. The hourly operational timescale of the respective maintenance tasks can be converted to quarterly and annual tasks, i.e.:

250 hours = complete tasks every three to four months.

500 hours = complete tasks every six months.

1,000 hours = complete tasks every year.

If a tractor is unused for prolonged periods the engine and transmission oil, fuel, tyre pressures, battery and grease points should be checked regularly (once a month) to prevent deterioration of any fluids and parts.

Before carrying out any of the tasks always take care of your safety (see safety section on page 6) and familiarise yourself with the task as explained. After purchasing a second-hand tractor – even one that has been serviced beforehand – it is useful, especially for peace of mind, to carry out regular maintenance to maintain reliability. This will also confirm that previous maintenance has been performed correctly.

Before servicing your tractor it is necessary to obtain the parts that are likely to be required. By checking the service task chart you can list all the parts for a major (once a year) service. You also need to inspect the tractor to determine any additional parts required: often a quick visual inspection and drive will suffice.

All fluids and filters cannot be disposed of into normal domestic waste and must be taken to a recycling point or local dealer. Alternatively, if you find yourself accumulating a large amount of filters or fluid, drums can be supplied by waste recycling companies. This alternative will come at a cost, but it is cheaper than a fine!

Storage of the tractor over the winter period can be anything from a simple tarpaulin covering the machine in the corner of a field or side of a building to a dry, dust-free barn or garage. On tractors stored outside there will be damp and moisture implications for the following parts. Typical means of reducing or preventing moisture damage are explained below.

Seal exhaust - Use an old fizzy drink can, plastic bottle or thick plastic bag and an elastic band to secure the bag.

Seal air intake - Remove the pre-cleaner if possible and plug the pipe as above.

Battery - These do not like being left unused; therefore remove from the vehicle and keep fully charged by connecting to a small battery trickle charger until required. Store it away from sources of cold.

Brakes - Put the tractor in gear and chock the wheels to prevent the brakes seizing on.

Tyres - Cover to remove ultra violet light deterioration. Ensure the pressures are correct and replace any perished tyres.

Paint work - Repair any bare metal scratches with primer and top coat or paint with oil/penetrating fluid, ideally applying a wax coating spray to give the best protection.

To carry out a major service check the items listed on the service chart. (See page 24.)

The daily checks on the tractor are assumed to be carried out and therefore the next service interval is 50 hours. This interval consists of mainly additional top-ups and inspection. Greasing is one of the critical parts and this should be carried out at the end of the service so as to avoid covering yourself in grease when inspecting other parts of the tractor.

Grease points:
1. Front axle spindles
2. Steering drag link front joints
3. Front wheel bearing (if fitted)
4. Steering drag link rear joints
5. Levelling box
6. Lift rod levelling fork
7. Steering column top bearing
8. Brake pedal shaft.

3.01. Grease plan

Operator Maintenance

Service Chart

Task	every 10 hours	50	125	250	500	750	1000
Inspect for oil water and fuel leaks	daily check						
Check and top up engine oil level	daily check						
Top up fuel tank each evening to prevent condensation in fuel tank	daily check						
Air cleaner clean as conditions indicate	daily check						
Grease independent brake shaft bearings	X	X	X	X	X	X	X
Grease front axle swivel pins and steering connections	X	X	X	X	X	X	X
Grease levelling lever gearbox and thread	X	X	X	X	X	X	X
Check brake pedal free play	X	X	X	X	X	X	X
Check and adjust clutch pedal free play	X	X	X	X	X	X	X
Check and top up engine coolant level	X	X	X	X	X	X	X
Check and adjust tyre pressures	X	X	X	X	X	X	X
Check tightness of all wheel nuts/studs	X	X	X	X	X	X	X
Gearbox/rear axle oil level top up		X	X	X	X	X	X
Check fan belt tension		X	X	X	X	X	X
Drain fuel/water from diesel fuel filter housing		X	X	X	X	X	X
Check transmission oil level		X	X	X	X	X	X
Replace engine oil and filter			X	X	X	X	X
Grease steering box top bearing			X	X	X	X	X
Remove distributor cap and lubricate internal parts			X	X	X	X	X
Remove and check spark plug's condition and gap			X	X	X	X	X
Check and top up battery and clean terminals		X	X	X	X	X	X
Remove cover and wash out gauze filter in engine sump				X	X	X	X
Replace fuel filters (gravity fed system)				X	X	X	X
Lubricate front axle centre pivot pin				X	X	X	X
Clean internals of distributor cap and check cb points condition/gap				X	X	X	X
Lubricate dynamo commutator end bearing				X	X	X	X
Clean gauze filter in fuel sediment bowl			X	X	X	X	X
Check operation of injectors and service					X	X	X
Replace diesel fuel filters					X	X	X
Check engine valve clearances					X	X	X
Clean engine breather tube/filter					X	X	X
Drain and replace coolant antifreeze					X	X	X
Check and top up steering box oil						X	X
Grease water pump bearings						X	X
Replace gearbox and rear hydraulic oil						X	X
Repack rear axle bearings with grease							X
Check front axle hub, axle and steering for wear and adjustment							X
Check rubber boots on gear levers to prevent dirt and water ingress							X
Inspect dynamo commutator and brushes for wear							X
Drain fuel tank, remove and clean out							X
Replace front axle wheel bearing grease							X

3.02. Engine oil level

3.02. With the vehicle on level ground and the engine stationary for at least 10 minutes, withdraw the engine oil dipstick and wipe with a clean cloth. Insert it back in the dipstick tube then remove and with the stick pointing towards the ground check the oil mark is between the maximum and minimum lines. (See page 21.)

3.03. Radiator coolant level

3.03. Remove the radiator cap only if it feels cold: a hot engine will allow expanding coolant to scald you. Slowly turn the cap and allow any pressure to escape. The coolant level should be just below the filler neck of the cap housing. With the cap removed check its rubber seal for damage (as shown in the picture).

3.04. Check tyre pressures

3.04. Using a pump pressure gauge check and adjust tyre pressures. Front tyres should be 26 psi and rear tyres should be 12 psi; increase front pressure to 30 psi if using a loader.

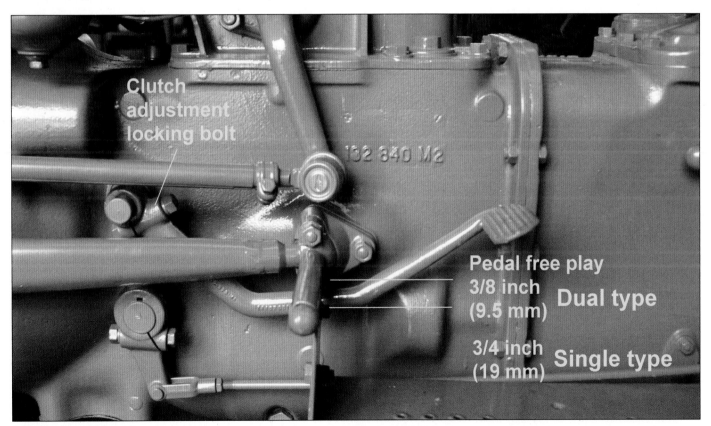

3.05. Clutch pedal free play

3.05. Clutch pedal free play must be checked regularly, especially if the tractor is used for loader work as this wears the clutch more quickly. Push down the pedal with your hand until a slight resistance is felt and then measure the movement of the pedal. See picture for clearance depending upon clutch type fitted. Any adjustment is carried out by slackening the clamp and turning the square shaft to reduce free play. Always maintain free play to prevent accelerated clutch wear.

3.06. Adjust rear brakes

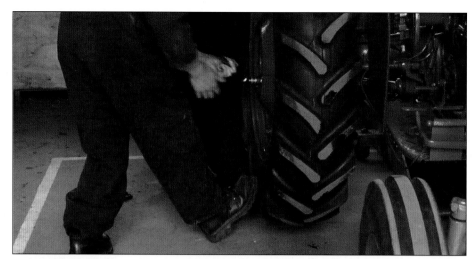

3.07. Tighten wheel nuts

3.08. Gearbox oil level

3.10. Fuel filters drain water

3.09. Fan belt tension

3.06. If the brake action feels poor or too much pedal travel is experienced, then the brakes required checking and/or adjusting. See Chapter 9 for brake repairs. Road test by travelling in second gear at half engine revs and gently applying the brakes, the tractor should steer in a straight line. If it pulls to one side or the other, slacken off the side it steers to and retest.

3.07. The wheel nuts should be checked regularly to prevent damage to the wheel centres and for safety. See service specification data on page 30.

3.08. With the vehicle on level ground and the engine stationary for at least 10 minutes, withdraw the transmission oil dipstick on the right-hand side casing and wipe with a clean cloth. Insert it back in the dipstick tube then remove and, with the stick pointing towards the ground, check the oil mark is between the maximum and minimum lines. If it requires topping up, fill from the plug by the gear levers but allow time for the oil to drain into the rear hydraulic casting before rechecking the level.

3.11. Drain engine oil

3.12. Layout of oil filter parts

3.09. Generator/fan belt condition must be checked for signs of cracking or perishing. If any signs are visible, replace by slackening dynamo and passing the belt over the fan blades and pulleys. Check the length with new belt and refit to engine. Re-tension the belt using the movement of the generator bracket. Recheck after 10 hours (1 day) operation to allow for stretching of the new belt.

3.10. Condensation will accumulate in the diesel tank and form water droplets. It is necessary to drain this damaging liquid by unscrewing the drain cock at the bottom of the first filter (grey). Then slacken off the bleed screw and prime the filter with fresh diesel by operating the hand primer lever on the lift pump. If air enters the system you may have to bleed the fuel system to allow the engine to start. (See Chapter 6 for more information on fuel systems.)

3.11. To replace the engine oil, operate the tractor until it reaches normal running temperature. Take care when draining the hot oil and wear suitable gloves to prevent burning your hands. You will need a container that is large enough to accommodate the volume of oil, which could amount to 12 pints (or 6.8 litres).

3.12. When refitting the paper element filter keep the parts in order. When filling the engine with fresh oil, remember to replace the sump plug first and, if possible, top up to the middle of the oil filter to enable oil pressure to build quickly on start up.

Once the correct amount of oil has been added to the sump, crank over the engine with the fuel stop out or ignition disconnected (to prevent the engine starting). Continue until oil pressure is registered on gauge, then start the engine and run for 2-3 minutes. Then check for leaks around the oil filter and sump plug; stop the engine and wait for 5 minutes before checking the level on the dipstick.

3.13. Points and distributor cap

3.13. An engine fitted with spark ignition relies on the production of a good spark! This can be achieved by checking that the distributor cap, leads and rotor arm are clean. It also helps to lubricate the centre shaft with a drop of engine oil.

3.14. Remove the plug leads, noting their positions, and then unscrew the spark plugs using a spark plug socket. Check the colour of the plug tips: they should be light beige. See page 182 Electrics section for colour explanation of plug condition. Check the gap using a feeler gauge. This should be between 0.78 and 0.81 mm (0.031 – 0.032 in).

3.14. Remove spark plugs

3.15. Check battery condition

3.16. Removing sump strainer

3.17. Check cb points

3.15. Before topping up the battery check its condition using a hydrometer, which will measure the specific gravity or relative density of the liquid and will tell you if one or more of the cells are going to fail and let you down in the winter. To top up, fill the battery with distilled water to the maximum mark inside the battery cell or just above the plates viewed through the hole in the cover. Tip: if the weather is cold, charge up your battery afterwards to prevent freezing of liquid.

3.16. Remove the sump oil strainer and wash out to clean the gauze. Then fit

a new gasket and use a silicon sealer to refit the cleaned strainer to the sump, tightening the nuts evenly.

3.17. Remove the distributor cap and check the condition of the contact breaker points. They must be free from oil or grease and not burned or blackened. Using a piece of fine emery paper open the points and clean the surfaces. To check the gap turn the engine until the cam opens the points and then check the gap using a feeler gauge.

3.18. Remove the rubber bung from the rear of the dynamo and use an oil can to

lubricate the commutator end bearing with a few drops.

3.19. Remove the cover of the fuel lift pump and extract the fine gauze filter. Wash out with brake cleaner spray or clean fuel. Using an air line carefully blow out the dirt in the lift pump housing then replace the filter and refit the cover, ensuring the seal is fitted correctly.

3.20. Using an antifreeze hydrometer, check the strength of the mixture. It is advisable to maintain at least 33% (5 pints or 3 litres) and replace this every

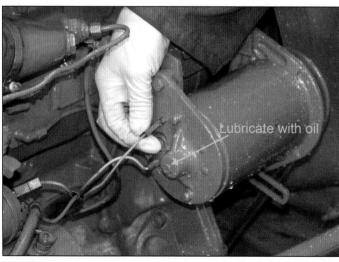

3.18. Lubricate dynamo rear bearing

3.19. Clean fuel lift pump filter

3.20. Antifreeze test

two years to maintain anti-corrosion strength.

3.21. Top up the steering box to the filler/level plug with tractor universal oil. A common filler plug on the steering box casting serves both the transmission and hydraulic oil. Remember to allow time for the oil to drain into the rear hydraulic casting where the dipstick is situated on the right-hand inspection cover.

3.22. To drain transmission and hydraulic oils remove the two drain plugs in the bottom of the castings; ensure that you have a container large enough to cope with 30 litres of oil!

3.23. To replenish the antifreeze open the drain taps on the block and the bottom of the radiator and collect the old fluid. Remember to dispose of this fluid correctly as it is very harmful to the environment. Flush the cooling system with clean water and then refill with the recommended mixture of antifreeze and clean water.

3.24. Check the rubber boots on the gear levers to ensure that they are free from ingress, water or dirt and that the gear levers are free to move. Apply a few drops of oil into the sockets before replacing the boots.

3.21. Steering and gearbox filler plugs

3.22. Drain transmission oil

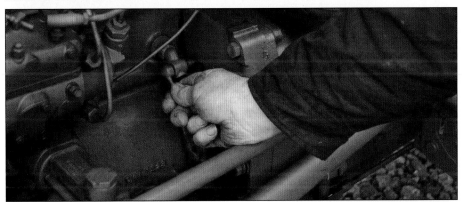

3.23. Drain coolant

3.24. Gear lever play and rubber boots

3.25. Grease rear linkage

3.26. Check injectors

3.27. Change fuel filter

3.28. Remove fuel tank and clean

3.25. Grease the rear hydraulic linkage to ensure smooth operation.

3.26. Periodically the fuel injectors should be removed and tested to ensure correct spray pattern and opening pressures. This will help to maintain good starting and performance from the engine.

3.27. The fuel filters should be replaced at the recommended set intervals to maintain efficient operation of the fuel injection components and to prevent premature wear. Make sure all the relevant seals are replaced to prevent leaks and air ingress.

3.28. Allow the fuel level to drop to a minimum, disconnect fuel pipe and then remove the battery and rear fuel tank bolts. Slacken the two front nuts and slide the tank rearward. Using clean fuel, wash out the tank to remove any corrosion, water or sludge deposits.

Service Specification Data

Description	Specification
Engine sump petrol and diesel	6.8 litres (12 pints)
Air cleaner bowl	0.43 litres (¾ pint)
Transmission	30.28 litre (6.6 Imp gallons)
Steering gearbox	0.95 litres (1.8 pints)
Cooling system diesel 23C	8.5 litres (15 pints)
Cooling system diesel 3A.152	5.96 litres (10.5 pints)
Cooling system petrol/TVO	8.5 litres (15 pints)
Valve clearance. Inlet & exhaust 3A.152	0.30 mm (0.012 in) cold
Valve clearance. Inlet 23C and 87 mm	0.30 mm (0.012 in) cold
Valve clearance. Exhaust 23C and 87 mm	0.203 mm (0.008 in) cold
Spark plug gap	0.76 to 0.81 mm (0.030 to 0.032 in)
Contact breaker points gap	0.36 to 0.41 mm (0.014 to 0.016 in)
Front tyre pressure	1.8 bar (26 psi)
Rear tyre pressure	0.8 bar (12 psi)
Clutch free play dual type	9.5 mm (⅜ in)
Clutch free play single type	19 mm (¾ in)
Front wheel nuts torque	76 to 83 Nm (55-60 lb-ft)
Rear wheel nuts torque	124 to 138 Nm (90-100 lb-ft)
Fan belt deflection	19 mm (¾ in)

Description	Fluid Specification
Engine sump A3.152 3-cylinder diesel	Super tractor universal oil (mineral) 20W/40 or 15W/30
Engine sump 23c 4-cylinder diesel	Super tractor universal oil (mineral) 20W/40 or 15W/30
Engine sump 87 mm Petrol/TVO	Super tractor universal oil (mineral) 20W/40 or 15W/30
Air cleaner bowl	Super tractor universal oil (mineral) 20W/40 or 15W/30
Transmission	Super tractor universal oil (mineral) 20W/40 or 15W/30
Steering gearbox	Super tractor universal oil (mineral) 20W/40 or 15W/30
Cooling system	Universal mono-ethylene glycol antifreeze
Grease	Multi-purpose EP2 grease

Chapter 4 Engines

This chapter deals with the engine variations fitted to Massey Ferguson 35 tractors. First we cover the 4-cylinder 23c diesel engine as fitted to the grey and gold tractors and the early FE35 tractors. Then the 4-cylinder 87 mm Petrol/TVO (Tractor Vaporising Oil) engines and finally the 3-cylinder 3.152 diesel engines fitted from serial number 165596 in 1959.

One of the problems with reusing the old engine block is the effort required to strip down the engine and then, when reassembling the parts, cleanliness is extremely important to achieve reliability. Hence all the parts must be thoroughly cleaned with every trace of old oil, sludge and dirt removed before any reassembly can take place. Degreasing agents such as paraffin-based fluid or even heating oil will break down the build up of grime and then a pressure washer, or even better a steam cleaner, can be used to finally remove the residue.

(Note, be careful where the old oil and cleaning fluid runs off as you must not allow it to enter a drain or water course.) At each stage of the rebuild, rotate the components to make sure that they are running smoothly and have not been fitted incorrectly. Taking pictures at critical stages of the disassembly can help in an hour of need, especially as reassembly may be many months later!

The cylinder head and valve components, springs, collars and caps are removed and placed in a valve stand tray to keep them safe and in fitment order. After thoroughly cleaning the cylinder head gasket surface using wet and dry paper and decoking it (to remove the carbon deposits) with wire drill attachments we can now recondition the unit.

Specialist valve seat cutting equipment is required to cut the seats but this can be quite cost prohibitive unless you intend to work on several engines. Therefore a specialist engine re-conditioner should be used to carry out the work. If the valve guides are found to be worn they will need to be removed by using a press and a machined guide tool. When new valves are fitted then all the free play will be removed.

To ensure the new pistons are fitted in the correct orientation only swap one at a time. Remove the old circlips and slide out the gudgeon pin, fit the con rod onto the new piston and use the new circlips which come with the pistons. Check the small end bush movement in the new gudgeon pin, any appreciable play will necessitate fitting new bushes,

and ream to fit (by a machine shop). The new piston rings are supplied in sets and are packaged to ensure the correct position on the piston. Note some rings have to be fitted with the word 'TOP' facing the piston crown because of the shape of the ring face. Always use a piston ring expander to prevent breakages.

Any scoring or marks on the crankshaft journal faces should be removed through regrinding by a specialist reconditioning company. Oversized shell bearings will need to be used when refitting the crankshaft to the engine to take into account the material removed by regrinding. The sizes required will be provided by the engine reconditioner after the regrinding.

TIGHTENING TORQUES for 4-cylinder 23c diesel engine

	Nm		lb-ft	
Bearing Housing to Block—Centre	52.90	56.97	39	42
Bearing Housing to Block—Front	24.42	27.12	18	20
Bearing Housing—Upper to Lower	33.90	40.70	25	39
Bearing Housing (Rear) and Cover Attachment	24.42	27.12	18	20
Camshaft Chain Wheel to Centre	24.42	27.12	18	20
Clutch Attachment— Single	35.27	37.97	26	28
Clutch Attachment—Dual	29.84	32.55	22	24
Connecting Rod Bolts	88.16	94.94	65	70
Cylinder Head—Manifolds	29.84	32.55	22	24
Injectors	16.27	18.99	12	14
Rocker Shaft Oil Feed	21.70	24.42	16	18
Cylinder Head Attachment to Block	135.67	142.45	100	105
Dynamo Bracket to Cylinder Block	24.42	27.12	18	20
Dynamo Mounting	35.27	37.97	26	28
Dynamo to Bracket	24.42	27.12	18	20
Exhaust Pipe Attachment	29.84	32.55	22	24
Fan Hub to Water Pump Spindle — Nyloc Nut	21.70	24.42	16	18
— $\frac{5}{10}$ UNF Nut	16.27	18.99	12	14
Fan Pulley to Hub	24.42	27.12	18	20
Flywheel Attachment	122.07	133.71	90	100
Fuel Pump Attachment	16.27	18.99	12	14
Injector Pump Drive Casing to Block — Setscrew	24.42	27.12	18	20
— Bolt	21.70	24.42	16	18
Injection Pump Mounting	29.84	32.55	22	24
Injector Clamp	24.42	27.12	18	20
Oil Filter to Cylinder Block	35.27	37.97	26	28
Oil Pump Attachment	21.70	24.42	16	18
Oil Pump to Front Bearing Housing	16.27	18.99	12	14
Oil Suction Pipe Bracket to Cylinder Block	24.42	27.12	18	20
Oil Sump Attachment — Bolts and Setscrews	21.70	24.42	16	18
— Nut	18.99	21.70	14	16
Rocker Cover and Pedestal	4.07	6.78	3	5
Rocker Pedestal	29.84	32.55	22	24
Rocker Shaft to Pedestal	10.85	13.57	8	10
Starter Motor Attachment to Cylinder Block	50.19	54.25	37	40
Tappet Cover Attachment	24.42	27.12	18	20
Thermostat—Elbow to Thermostat Body and Body to Cylinder Head	24.42	27.12	18	20
Timing Cover	24.42	27.12	18	20
Timing Chain Tensioner Attachment	10.85	13.57	8	10
Water Pump Attachment	29.84	32.55	22	24
Water Pump Attachment to Cylinder Block	35.27	37.97	26	28

MF 35 4-cylinder 23c Diesel Engine Overhaul

🔧 Tools required for checks:

Range of imperial spanners and ⅜,
½ and ¾ drive socket sets

Flat and Philips blade screwdrivers

Hammer and small chisel

Valve stand tray

Trolley jack(s) and axle stands

Wooden wedges

Drain pans

Parts containers and masking tape

Protective gloves

It is important that the various common components can be reassembled in the correct (same) position and to this end trays or boxes must be used to keep the components arranged in order of disassembly.

To begin the process of stripping the engine, first remove the cylinder head and sump. Remember to drain the engine oil and antifreeze. As we are stripping the tractor completely we will have already removed the major components, e.g. radiator and air cleaner housing, which provides easier access to the engine components.

In order to allow for a complete strip down of the engine and removal of the crankshaft, it is necessary to lift the engine from the chassis frame. It is easier on this model to split the engine away from the gearbox at the bell housing.

To remove the cylinder head and pistons follow the pictorial procedure:

4.01. Battery disconnect

4.01. Disconnect the battery leads first. Remove the earth lead and then the live lead to prevent any short circuits and sparks. Before disconnecting any of the wiring, label each connection point.

4.02. & 4.03. Disconnect the following to remove the cylinder head:

A. Leak off return pipe in tank.
B. Turn off fuel tap and remove pipe to lift pump.
D. Remove two battery tray bolts at the rear of fuel tank.
E. Slacken off the front spring loader tank bolt lock nuts, slide tank rearwards and lift away.
F. Remove bypass hose.
G. Remove injector pipes and seal ends.
H. Remove injector leak off pipe.
I. Remove radiator top hose.
C. Remove thermostat fuel lines and lift unit away.
J. Remove air intake hose.
K. Remove exhaust pipe at joint.
L. Remove engine breather pipe at rocker cover.

4.02. Left-hand view

4.03. Right-hand view

4.04. Radiator drain

4.05. Radiator off

4.06. Rocker cover off

4.07. Injector removal

4.08. Rocker shaft off

4.04. Screw in the radiator drain tap and collect the antifreeze in a suitable container that is capable of holding about 4 litres. Then screw in the engine block drain tap and collect antifreeze in a suitable container that is capable of holding about 4.5 litres.

4.05. Once the fluid has been drained, remove the top and bottom hoses. Then remove the top tie rod and lower mounting nuts, ensuring that you keep safe the front axle casing to radiator rubber mounting blocks.

4.06. Remove engine breather pipe hose from the rocker cover. Then remove the rocker cover nuts and washers and gently lift off the cover, retrieving the old cork gasket.

4.07. Mark each injector starting with number one at the water pump end of the engine (this is the standard numbering procedure for all rebuilds)

then slacken off the retaining nuts evenly, lift off the bridging pieces and gently prise the injectors out of the head. Make a note that the copper sealing washer will need to be removed from the hole once the cylinder head is off the engine.

4.08. Slacken the rocker shaft retaining nuts evenly starting from the centre outwards and gradually release the pressure, lift it off and place in the valve tray.

4.09. To keep the push rods in the correct order lift out each rod in turn and place in the valve stand. Alternatively, use a stiff piece of card with holes numbered one to eight for each push rod.

4.10. Remove each valve stem tip cap and keep in order using an old weekly pill tray. Note: the larger caps fit the exhaust valves and the smaller ones the inlet valves.

4.09. Push rods removed

4.10. Remove valve caps

4.11. Head removal sequence

4.12. Lift head off

4.13. Remove sump

4.11. Slacken the cylinder head bolts and nuts in the order shown. Unscrew each by a quarter of a turn and then repeat until they are all slack.

4.12. Remove the head bolts, nuts and flat washer and place them in the valve tray. Lift off the cylinder head with the thermostat housing attached; if necessary tap the corner of the head with a copper mallet or piece of wood to break the head gasket seal. If it will not loosen, check for a missed bolt or nut still attached.

4.13. To remove the sump, first drain the engine oil and then remove the nuts, securing the oil strainer from the left-hand side of the sump, and carefully pull it out. Remove the 20 bolts retaining the sump including the ones on the gearbox clutch (bell) housing. Note: the front axle is supported by the sump and therefore has to be removed.

Support the tractor using the flat surface plate under the clutch (bell) housing with a small axle stand. Gently tap the sump to break the gasket seal and use a small trolley jack to support the weight of the sump.

4.14. Closer inspection of the bores reveals a marked wear ridge in the top section of the liner as shown by the silver line and black line. The extent of the wear will be measured in the engine assessment.

4.15. As was suspected after the low compression reading obtained on the first inspection and the constant misfire, the number four cylinder top piston ring had broken and decided to 'eat' its way out of the piston and embed itself in the piston crown. The big end bearings have worn away the white (grey) metal bearing material to reveal the copper backing layer. Not good!

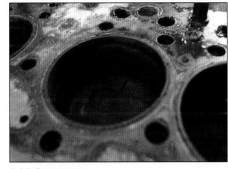

4.14. Bore wear

4.15. Misfire reason

Engine condition inspection

A special tool consisting of a flat plate with two holes drilled to match the flywheel holes with a metal lifting loop attached is required to withdraw the crankshaft, including the main bearing housing, from the engine. This tool is easy to manufacture. A suitable lifting hoist or crane will make life easier by preventing damage to the components as well as trapped fingers!

It is crucial that the engine components are marked to allow for ease of reassembly and to ensure they are refitted in the correct position or order. Centre punch dot marks and/or manufacturer's marking will help to achieve this as it may be several weeks, if not months, before the parts are refitted.

With the engine finally stripped down, we can assess the condition of the components.

At this stage it always helps to have a knowledgeable friend to offer advice on parts that require replacement or reconditioning. However, you could work on the 'if in doubt, throw it out' principle.

You must not skimp on replacing parts because in the long term any shortcuts or economies will inevitably reduce the life and reliability of the engine.

Engine overhaul kits include most of the parts required to repair the engine block and cylinder head. The tractor that is the subject of the photographs was difficult to start, low on power and produced excessive blue smoke so it is safe to assume that the internal components – such as the pistons, rings, bores and bearings – are well past their best and will definitely need replacing. Wear measurements are given to allow the reader to make their own judgements.

🔧 Tools required for checks:

Range of imperial spanners and ⅜, ½ and ¾ drive socket sets

11 mm (⁷⁄₁₆ in) socket screw

Flat and Philips blade screwdrivers

Hammer and a small chisel

Valve stand tray

Piston ring expanders

Lifting chain and crane

Feeler gauge

Pry bars

Parts containers and masking tape

Protective gloves

To remove the crankshaft with ancillaries, including wear assessment, follow the pictorial procedure:

4.16. Remove clutch and flywheel

4.16. Unlike the 3-cylinder MF 35 tractor (which requires safety bolts to be fitted to the clutch cover before removal from the flywheel) the 4-cylinder 23c engine clutch can be removed by evenly slackening the bolts on the periphery of the clutch. The flywheel is removed by bending back the locking tabs and removing the set screws. Note: the extra hole to correctly align the timing marks.

4.17. Before the crankshaft and timing chain can be removed from the block, the oil pump assembly must be extracted as this is part of the front main bearing housing. Use a punch to remove the pin and drive gear and take out the four bolts while retaining the pump body. Note: the top right-hand bolt looking from the front of the engine is the master locating bolt and should be refitted in this position to ensure alignment of the pump shaft bushes.

4.17. Oil pump gear

4.18. Timing marks

4.19. Lever off gears

4.20. Injector pump off

4.21. Oil pump housing and front bearing

4.18. Before removing the timing gears and chain ensure the timing marks can be identified as the lines are very faintly scored. Remove the crankshaft front pulley woodruff key and shims, then check that the camshaft front flange and sprocket have 'centre pop' marks (shown by the letter 'a') in order that the camshaft timing is correct when refitted.

4.19. Remove the timing chain tensioner. Then remove the six camshaft retaining bolts and lever the lower sprocket off the crankshaft.

4.20. Remove the injector pump, but first ensure the scribe line on the pump has a corresponding line on the pump drive housing. Lift away the pump and remove the short quill shaft from the housing. Then unbolt the drive housing from the side of the engine. Keep the old gasket as its thickness determines the gear mesh with the camshaft gear.

4.21. Remove the bolts securing the front main bearing housing and withdraw from the engine block. Note that the rear gasket will need to be replaced.

4.22. Remove the rear main bearing housing bolts and the housing with the gasket and rear crankshaft seal. Both of these will need to be replaced when refitting the housing. Invert the engine as shown and place the fabricated bracket to the end of the crankshaft. Unscrew the centre main bearing locating bolt. Finally, use a hoist or crane to lift out the crankshaft.

4.23. Once on the bench the centre and rear main bearing housings can be stripped and the crankshaft journals inspected for suitability of reuse. Note that the rear housing also incorporates the crankshaft seal.

4.24. The crankshaft's main shell bearing (left of picture) reads 020 U/S (or 0.020 in Under/ Size). This means that at some point in the engine's life the crank has been reground and oversized shells fitted. As the crank journal surfaces are scored we can grind to the next size of 0.030 in. Similarly, the big end shell (right of picture) reads 010, which indicates that a 0.010 in oversized shell bearing has been used to compensate for the regrinding.

4.25. Typical crankshaft journal faults include scored marks and scuff marks which will require regrinding of the crankshaft journals.

4.26. The shell bearing has picked up and consequently scored the crankshaft journal very badly. Unfortunately this crankshaft cannot be reground and is now scrap.

4.22. Lift out crank

4.23. Crank strip

4.24. Crank bearings

4.25. Crank wear 1

4.26. Crank wear 2

4.27. The main shell bearing oil groove can be clearly identified, this gives an indication of the amount of wear on the journal surface. With any assessment of the journal if your fingernail can pick up any grooves or ridges then the crankshaft will need polishing or regrinding prior to the fitting of the new bearings.

4.27. Crank wear 3

4.28. To remove scoring, out of roundness and blemishes on the crankshaft journal surfaces a special lathe/grinder is utilised that produces a perfectly round and smooth mirror finish. New shell bearings (which are not included in the engine overhaul kit) will be required. These are available in three different thicknesses depending upon the amount of metal that needs to be ground off the bearing journals to make them good. These should be ordered after the regrind.

4.28. Crank wear refurbish

4.29. If you are hoping to reuse the original piston rings, they must be checked for wear of the periphery edge, which is in contact with the cylinder bore of the engine. To do this, carefully remove the piston rings (ideally with a ring expander), place one in the top of the unworn part of the bore and measure the gap using a feeler gauge. The limit is 0.737 mm (0.029 in).

To assess if the cylinder bore is worn feel the lip at the top of the bore with your fingernail. If the ridge is pronounced (usually 0.152–0.254 mm/0.006–0.010 in) it needs to be replaced. If the piston rings are worn past their limits then usually the bore will be as well.

4.29. Piston ring end gap

4.30. Piston ring groove

4.31. Oil pump wear

4.30. If you are anticipating using the old piston rings, then the ring groove in the piston needs to be checked. With a new piston ring inserted into the relevant groove, use a feeler gauge to measure the clearance, the limit is 0.155 mm (0.0061 in). This limit is essential: too large a clearance will allow the rings to 'flutter' and cause breakages and/or rapid groove wear.

4.31. To ensure the long life of a new engine always fit a new oil pump on the rebuild. If you wish to use the old one and the pump rotor edges are not scored then check the operating clearance using a feeler gauge between the peaks of the inner and outer rotors. The limit is 0.254 mm (0.010 in).

Engine rebuild

Now that the crankshaft has been reground we will begin reassembling the engine's components. In anticipation we ordered the next size of mains and big end shell bearings. Unfortunately, when the crank was previously reground the front end spigot was not checked for parallel alignment and when it was machined it caused the journals to be ground out of alignment. In order to fix this problem, the part required further grinding to bring the crankshaft back in alignment; it also meant that the largest thickness of shell bearings had to be ordered. This means the crank cannot be machined again and this is possibly one of the reasons that the shell bearings wore rapidly. It is always important to find a machine shop with the skills and knowledge to produce quality workmanship.

Our attention turned to the cylinder head. Previously we removed all the valve components – springs, collars and caps – and placed them in a valve stand tray to keep them safe and in order of fitment. After thoroughly cleaning the head and decoking it with wire drill bits we can

🔧 Tools required for checks:

Steam cleaner	Piston ring compressor
Range of imperial spanners and ⅜ and ½ drive sockets	Hydraulic press
	Heated water bath
7 mm (⁷⁄₁₆ in) socket screw	Lifting chain and crane
Torque wrench	Feeler gauge
Hammer and a small chisel	Straight edge
Valve seat cutting equipment (Neway)	Gasket sealer
	Dial gauge
Wire brushes and air drill	Vernier calipers
Piston ring expanders	

now recondition the unit. Specialist valve-cutting equipment is required which can be cost prohibitive unless you are working on several engines. Further, a hydraulic press is required to fit the new valve guides, therefore it may be cheaper to entrust the reconditioning to a local machine shop.

As our engine is renowned for poor starting we must ensure that the engine is rebuilt to the manufacturer's tolerances and limits in order to retain the highest compression within the cylinder for ease of starting. This will also ensure that the tractor has a long, reliable working life.

When reassembling, cleanliness of the parts is extremely important to achieve reliability. All parts must be thoroughly cleaned with every trace of old oil, sludge and dirt removed before any reassembly can take place. At each stage of the rebuild, it is advisable to rotate the components to make sure that they are running smoothly and that they have been fitted correctly. Taking pictures during disassembly may prove invaluable in an hour of need, especially given that reassembly may take place many months later!

To rebuild the engine assembly follow the pictorial procedure:

4.32. Clean the parts

4.33. Re-cut valve seats

4.34. Lapping in the valves

4.35. Valve face depth

4.32. The cylinder head required decoking; this means removing all the soot and carbon deposits within the ports of the head. A small wire brush attached to a drill makes the job easier.

4.33. The valve seats are cut to 15 degrees top angle, 45 degrees seat angle and 60 degrees bottom angle. This ensures a narrow-width seat for the valve face and achieves excellent sealing.

4.34. By using fine grinding paste and a suction stick the valve seat and face are matched together by rotating the stick and applying a downward force. When a faint grey line appears on both surfaces, the sealing can be checked (after fitting valve springs, etc.) by filling the ports with diesel or paraffin and looking for the leaks. If these are evident, then further grinding will be necessary.

4.35. To ensure maximum engine compression the valves must not sink into the cylinder head by more than 2.54 mm (0.1 in) as this increases the volume above the piston, which leads to poor cold starting. If the seat has sunk because of wear then new seat inserts must be fitted by a machine shop.

4.36. Clean gasket surface

4.37. Check flatness

4.38. Refit new valves

4.36. To permit the head gasket to seal, the faces of the block and cylinder head must be clean of dirt and carbon. Using wet and dry emery paper on a block of hard wood gives a good finish.

4.37. A machined straight edge is used to check the cylinder head surface flatness with a feeler gauge. Approximately 0.15 mm (0.006 in) distortion before machining is required. The straight edge can also be utilised to check the valve face below the head surface as shown.

4.38. If the valves have excessive sideways movement in the cylinder head then the valve guides need to be replaced. They cannot be punched out as this will damage the guides. A mandrel machined to fit the guide is required and a hydraulic press will need to be used to remove and refit them. The protrusion from the rocker cover gasket surface to the top of the valve guide should measure as follows: inlets 12.7 mm (0.5 in) and exhausts 8.128 mm (0.32 in).

4.39. Before fitting the new liners, clean the internal surfaces of the bores to ensure a clean sliding fit. Pay particular attention to

4.39. Clean bore face

4.40. Liner step out

4.41. Rear end bearing

4.42. Centre bearing

the top ridge. Gently push in the liners with clean engine oil, but do not allow them to drop as this could damage the top flange.

4.40. Measure the top flange stand out. This must be between 0.25 and 0.076 mm (0.001 to 0.003 in) to ensure that the liner is 'nipped' by the head gasket and cylinder head when refitting.

4.41. To ensure the shell bearings are located by the notches in the housing, place the thrust washers with the oil grooves facing outwards onto the housings using grease. Fit the small rubber seals with a small amount of silicon sealer and bolt the two halves together, tightening to 35–42 Nm (25–30 lb-ft).

4.42. Fit new main bearings to the centre housing and torque bolts to 35–42 Nm (25–30 lb-ft). Ensure the offset centre bolt hole faces towards the rear of the engine.

4.43. Lower the crankshaft into the engine block. Fit the centre locating bolt, aligning the holes carefully to prevent cross threading. Tighten to 53–58 Nm (39–42 lb-ft).

4.43. Locating bolt

4.44. Fitting rear seal

4.45. Front bearing fit

4.46. Check crank end float

4.47. Heating pistons

4.44. Apply silicon sealer to both sides of the rear housing gasket. Ensure the holes are aligned; this will be tricky because of the offset machining. Note: the rear housing drain holes are facing the sump. Apply oil to the seal and carefully fit and tighten the bolts to 25 to 28 Nm (18 to 20 lb-ft).

4.45. Ensure the front gasket is aligned with the bolt holes and that sealer is applied. Carefully align housing into the block and torque the bolts to 25 to 28 Nm (18 to 20 lb-ft). Note: some of the bolts

retain the chain tensioner and oil pump.

4.46. Check that the crank is free to rotate with minimum drag; it should be possible to turn by hand. Check the crankshaft end float with a dial gauge mounted on a magnetic base. The reading should be 0.152–0.203 mm (0.006–0.008 in). If they are found to be outside the limits, fit thicker thrust washers to the rear housing to compensate.

4.47. The gudgeon pins are a sliding fit in the piston when the engine is

at operating temperature, but tight when cold. To allow ease of removing the piston from the con rod they must be heated up in hot water. This also applies to the new pistons.

4.48. To ensure the new pistons are fitted in the correct orientation only swap one at a time. Remove the old circlips and slide out the gudgeon pin, fit the con rod onto the new piston and use the new circlips which come with the pistons. Check the small end bush movement in the new gudgeon pin –

4.48. Fitting new pistons

4.49. Piston rings fit

4.50. Rings gapped

4.51. Assembled internals

any appreciable play will necessitate fitting new bushes. Have a machine shop ream to fit.

4.49. The new piston rings are supplied in sets and are packaged to ensure the correct position on the piston. Note that some rings have to be fitted with the word 'TOP' facing the piston crown because of the shape of the ring face. Always use a piston ring expander to prevent breakages.

4.50. Note: the bottom ring is not used on this engine as it was found to lead to rapid engine bore wear.

With all the rings fitted, stagger the rings so that the gaps are 180 degrees apart. Apply copious amounts of clean engine oil and fit the piston ring compressor. When fitting to the engine, lubricate the engine bore and crank journal, gently tap into the respective bores (as marked on the con rod end).

Apply locking compound to the con rod bolts and torque to 88 to 95 Nm (65 to 70 lb-ft). Finally, bend over the lock tabs.

4.51. The first stage of the rebuild sees the new and reconditioned engine internal components refitted. Note the bolts and washers that are retaining the push fit liners to prevent them sliding out when rotating the engine due to the drag of the piston rings sliding up and down the bore.

Engine completed and first start up

As the engine comes together, we must ensure accurate assembly of the timing chain to maintain the exact timing of the valves opening and closing and the point when the fuel is injected into the engine in relation to the pistons. This will enable ease of starting and the engine will achieve optimum power.

When refitting the new oil pump, the internal inner and outer rotors are lubricated with clean engine oil, fitted

in the front bearing housing and then the outer housing cover fitted.

Note that the top right-hand bolt is shouldered and must be refitted to this position to locate the pump body. Refit the oil pump drive gears and check that the pump turns freely.

When fitting new gaskets ensure a suitable sealer is used, this will ensure the joint remains tight. Make sure you only apply enough sealer to form a thin layer, any excess will ooze out of the gap and this not only looks bad but also wastes the sealer; it will not seal any better.

🔧 Tools required for checks:

Steam cleaner

Range of imperial spanners and ⅜ and ½ drive sockets

7 mm (⁵⁄₁₆ in) socket screw

Torque wrench

Lifting crane and straps

Clutch aligning tool

Injector pop tester and tools

Tap and die set (Imperial)

Hammer and a small chisel

Wire brushes and air drill

Feeler gauge

Gasket sealer

To rebuild the engine assembly follow the pictorial procedure:

4.52. Timing marks

4.53. Timing tensioner

4.54. Pump drive master spline

4.55. Check timing marks

4.52. Fit the new timing chain to the camshaft sprocket and align the dot punch timing marks. Then fit the chain to the crankshaft sprocket and slide it onto the front spigot, ensuring that any brass shims have been refitted between the front end bearing housing and the crank sprocket beforehand: these shims are used to align the two sprockets. Next refit the camshaft bolts and tighten. Use a straight edge (hacksaw blade) to check the timing score marks are in line.

4.53. Keep the slack of the chain towards the chain tensioner mounting side. Fit the new tensioner, with the red tag kept in place, together with the distance plate between it and the engine block. Tighten the two bolts and remove the red tag, this should automatically activate the tensioner and the slipper pad will spring out and tension the chain.

4.54. With the timing marks aligned, turn the engine anticlockwise until the number one piston is halfway down the bore. Refit the flywheel with new lock tabs and ensure that the locating dowel in the crankshaft fits the flywheel. On the left-hand side of the engine is a small hole in the rear case; slide a 6.3 mm (¼ in) dowel into the casing, rotate the engine clockwise and the dowel should slide into a corresponding hole in the flywheel, locking the engine at 16 degrees before

4.56. Fit injection pump

Top Dead Centre (TDC). Fit the injection pump drive assembly onto the block (with a new gasket) and by turning the gear which is driven from the camshaft, position the master spline drive to approximately 45 degrees to the vertical.

4.55. Before we can fit the injection pump, the side inspection cover is removed to view the timing letter on the pump rotor. The letter 'G' should align with the line scribed on the internal circlip. Unfortunately ours did not so it was necessary to fit the pump to the 'pop' tester and by pressuring the outlet pipe to the number one injector, we can lock the pump into the correct position and make a timing mark on the circlip. It is advisable to

4.57. Timing cover fit

have this part of the procedure carried out by a fuel injection specialist if you do not have the necessary test equipment.

4.56. With the flywheel locating dowel fitted and the master spline on the pump drive at 45 degrees, the fuel injection pump with a new gasket can be fitted. Align the two scribed marks on the housing and the pump body. You should find the internal letter (G) will also be in the correct position with the internal circlip. Any adjustment can be made by rotating the pump slightly on the mounting flange.

4.57. Rotate the engine two revolutions and check that all the timing marks realign. Any slight adjustment can be made by

4.58. Fit sump

4.59. Oil pump strainer

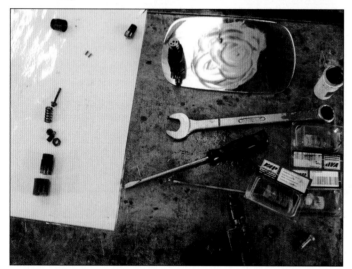

4.60. Injector overhaul

4.61. Water pump overhaul

rotating the injection pump body. Refit the inspection cover on the pump with a new gasket. Fit the timing cover with a new gasket and locate the cover on the dowels. Fit all the bolts loosely and then slide on the front pulley. Then tighten the bolts evenly. This procedure will align the new front seal with the front pulley to allow it to seal correctly.

4.58. Fit the oil pump pick-up pipe and apply sealer to the sump gasket. Lower the sump onto the block and fit all the various length bolts and tighten evenly. Note: the engine has been turned upside down to make working easier. Take care when turning it over the correct way as it is heavy.

4.59. Apply sealer to the new gasket and fit the oil pump strainer into the sump. Be careful not to over tighten the nuts as this will distort the thin housing and cause an oil leakage.

4.60. All the injectors are stripped down one at a time and the parts cleaned and replaced where necessary and then set up on a pop tester. Injector opening pressure is set to 130 bar. (See Diesel Engine Fuel Injectors section in Chapter 6 on page 105.)

4.62. Fitting the engine

4.63. Cleaning threads

4.64. Head gasket fit

4.61. To ensure the engine remains reliable all the ancillaries are replaced or overhauled. The water pump receives a new pump housing and gasket. Always mark the fan blades to prevent reversal refitment as this can cause the engine to overheat and is difficult to diagnose: the fan will 'blow' air through the radiator instead of 'suck'!

4.62. Finally, after all the hard work the engine is refitted to the rebuilt gearbox and the new clutch is aligned.

4.63. Before the cylinder head bolts and studs are refitted the threads are cleaned with a tap to prevent any possible damage and the holes are cleaned of any liquid or debris.

4.64. Clean the head and engine block gasket surfaces of oil, etc. Then fit the new head gasket taking note of the 'TOP' mark on one side of the gasket, this should face upwards. Do not apply any gasket sealer to the gasket as it is pre-fitted with a layer of special sealer.

4.65. Gently lower the cylinder head onto the engine block. Fit all the bolts and nuts with flat washers and tighten the bolts in the sequence illustrated by the numbers in the picture in three stages up to a final figure between 124 and 145 Nm (100 lb-ft).

4.65. Head torque procedure

4.66. Fit the valve stem tip caps: the large caps fit the exhausts and the smaller caps onto the inlets. Refit the push rods in their respective slots in the cylinder head. Fit the rocker shaft and locate each push rod onto each rocker end. Ensure you slacken each rocker, adjusting each screw before evenly tightening the pillar nuts. Be careful because if the valves make contact with the pistons they could get damaged.

Set the valve clearance using the 'Rule of Nine' procedure with the gaps adjusted to inlet valves 0.203 mm (0.008 in) and exhaust valves 0.305 mm (0.012 in) respectively. Turn the engine over slowly by turning the fan blade by hand or using the starting handle. Make sure that the fuel stop is out to prevent the engine running.

Watch the valves of one cylinder (i.e. number one cylinder) open and the opposite cylinder (i.e. number four cylinder) close in unison with each other. When one valve opens the rocker moves down and when the other one closes the rocker moves up. Set the valve clearances of the corresponding valves as shown in the Rule of Nine procedure.

4.66. Setting valve clearances

4.67. Connecting fuel lines

4.68. Rocker cover gasket

Rule of Nine	
Valve FULLY open	Check and adjust valve
Number 1 (nearest the radiator)	Number 8
Number 2	Number 7
Number 3	Number 6
Number 4	Number 5
Number 5	Number 4
Number 6	Number 3
Number 7	Number 2
Number 8	Number 1

4.67. The final task before starting the engine is to attach all the ancillaries, such as fuel lines, fuel lift pump, manifolds, water pump, thermostat housing and starter motor. Use a small 5-litre container to provide the diesel fuel. This will make the job easier because you will not have the hassle of fitting the diesel tank onto the top of the engine at this time.

The injector can now be fitted with new copper sealing washers and tightened evenly to 25–28 Nm (18–22 lb-ft).

4.68. Once the engine has reached operating temperature the cylinder head bolts will require re-checking and the valve clearances will need resetting due to metal expansion and contraction. To enable the rocker cover to be removed easily the cork gasket is only attached to the cover by a silicon sealer. This is allowed to cure before fitting to the cylinder head.

MF 35 4-cylinder 87 mm Petrol/TVO Engine Overhaul

The MF 35 engine is derived from the standard 85 mm unit used in the Ferguson TE-20 tractor, though it has increased power as a result of being bored out to 87 mm. The two engine units have quite a few parts in common, which makes them easier to locate.

The cylinder liners on the 4-cylinder (87 mm) engine are located in the engine block by the cylinder head; therefore, if the head is removed and the engine is turned, the liner could lift up and lose its lower sealing or allow the bottom piston ring to drop out. As this is the case, always fit washer/tubes on second and fourth head studs on the manifold side to secure the liners.

One of the problems with reusing the old engine block is the effort required to strip down the engine. As previously discussed, cleanliness is extremely important when reassembling parts. All parts must be thoroughly cleaned with every trace of old oil, sludge and dirt removed before reassembly. Degreasing agents such as paraffin-based fluid or even heating oil will break down the build up of grime at which point a pressure washer or, even better, a steam cleaner can be used to remove the residue.

Note: be careful where the old oil and cleaning fluid run off, you must not allow them to enter a drain or water course. As with the 4-cylinder 23c diesel engine, remember to rotate the components to make sure that they are running smoothly and have not been fitted incorrectly. It may help to take pictures at critical stages of the disassembly so that you have something to refer to at reassembly, which may be many months later!

When reconditioning the cylinder head, all the valve components, springs, collars and caps are removed and placed in a valve stand tray to keep them safe and in fitment order. After thoroughly cleaning the cylinder head gasket surface using wet and dry sandpaper and decoking it (to remove the carbon deposits) with wire drill attachments, the unit can be reconditioned.

Specialist valve seat cutting equipment is required to cut the seats but this can be quite cost prohibitive unless you intend to work on several engines. Therefore, a specialist engine reconditioner should be used to carry out the work. If the valve guides are found to be worn they will need to be removed by using a press and a machined guide tool. When new valves are fitted all the free play will be removed.

🔧 Tools required for checks:

Steam cleaner

Range of imperial spanners and ⅜ and ½ drive sockets

7 mm (⁵⁄₁₆ in) socket screw

Torque wrench

Hammer and a small chisel

Valve seat cutting equipment (Neway)

Wire brushes and air drill

Piston ring expanders

Piston ring compressor

Hydraulic press

Heated water bath

Lifting chain and crane

Feeler gauge

Straight edge

Gasket sealer

Dial gauge

Vernier calipers

Any scoring or marks on the crankshaft journal faces should be removed through regrinding by a specialist reconditioning company.

Oversized shell bearings will need to be used when refitting the crankshaft to the engine to take into account the material removed by regrinding. The required sizes will be provided by the engine reconditioner after the regrinding.

With all the ancillaries – such as the water pump, fuel injection pump, dynamo, flywheel and clutch – fitted, the engine is ready to be bolted back onto the tractor. Before starting the engine, fill with clean engine oil and ideally fit an accurate oil pressure gauge – if necessary use the dash-mounted gauge. Crank the engine over until the oil pressure has registered. Only then can the engine be started.

TIGHTENING TORQUES
for 87 mm petrol/TVO engine

	Nm		lb-ft	
Camshaft Locating Plate Attachment	24.89	— 27.65	18	— 20
Caps – Connecting Rod	69.13	— 76.04	50	— 55
Caps – Main Bearings	117.52	— 124.43	85	— 90
Clutch Attachment – Single	27.65	... ...	20	
Clutch Attachment – Dual	30.42	— 33.18	22	— 24
Rear Plate Cylinder Head	24.89	— 27.65	18	— 20
Cylinder Head	82.95	— 89.87	60	— 65
Dynamo Bracket to Cylinder Block	24.89	— 27.65	18	— 20
Dynamo to Bracket	24.89	— 27.65	18	— 20
Timing Cover	16.59	— 19.36	12	— 14
Fan and Pulley to Hub	24.89	— 27.65	18	— 20
Fan Pulley Hub to Water Pump Spindle	16.59	— 19.36	12	— 14
Gauze Filter to Sump	16.59	— 19.36	12	— 14
Flywheel Attachment to Crankshaft	58.07	— 63.60	42	— 46
Governor Attachment to Sprocket	11.06	— 13.83	8	— 10
Link to Dynamo	24.89	— 27.65	18	— 20
Manifold	30.42	— 33.18	22	— 24
Oil Filter Canister	30.42	— 33.18	22	— 24
Oil Filter Body to Block	24.89	— 27.65	18	— 20
Oil Pump	16.59	— 19.36	12	— 14
Rear Oil Seal Plates	11.06	— 13.83	8	— 10
Rocker Pedestal	30.42	— 33.18	22	— 24
Starter Motor Attachment	51.16	— 55.30	37	— 40
Sump to Block	22.12	— 24.89	16	— 18
Timing Chain Sprocket to Camshaft	30.41	— 33.18	22	— 24
Water Pump Bearing Housing to Body	30.42	— 33.18	22	— 24
Water Pump to Combustion Head	35.95	— 38.71	26	— 28

4.69. Disconnect ancillaries

The pictures demonstrate the areas of wear typically found in an old, worn out engine and the tasks required to restore it to a working condition.

4.69. Stripping the tractor engine and inspecting the internal parts is the only way to discover the cause of poor starting or loss of power from the engine. Remove the cylinder head and then the engine sump to gain access to the valves, pistons and bores. This will start to give you an inventory of repairs required. Mark the components with tape or white marker to aid reassembly.

4.70. Unbolt the 'U' clamp and allow the spring to slide off the throttle shaft. You can then slide the shaft out from under the dash panel.

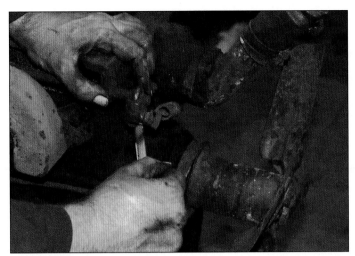

4.70. Remove governor linkage

4.71. Remove rocker shaft

4.72. Remove cylinder head nuts

4.73. Note position of washers on head

4.71. Remove the engine breather pipe banjo bolt and then remove the rocker cover nuts. Lift away the cover and then slacken off the rocker nuts evenly. Then remove the shaft and carefully take off and store the caps on the valve stems. Lift out the push rods and keep in order.

4.72. Slacken the head nuts ¼ of a turn at a time in the order of tightening (See picture on page 66.)

4.73. When removing the nuts take note of the various washers fitted to the cylinder head.

4.74. With the cylinder head nuts removed, the back heat shield for the TVO engine operation can be lifted away.

4.74. Lift off heat shield

4.75. Remove head

4.76. Gasket failure

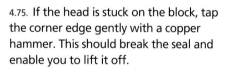

4.77. Remove sump

4.78. Remove front pulley

4.79. Governor plate

4.80. Camshaft marks

4.75. If the head is stuck on the block, tap the corner edge gently with a copper hammer. This should break the seal and enable you to lift it off.

4.76. Close inspection of the head gasket reveals burning between the bores because of a leaking radiator. This could possibly be causing the engine to overheat.

4.77. In order to remove the sump, first remove the gauze filter from the right-hand side of the sump and then take out all the set bolts. Note the sludge in the bottom of the sump due to poor maintenance.

4.81. Camshaft thrust plate

4.82. Camshaft out

4.83. Bend back locking tabs

4.84. Push out pistons

4.78. To remove the timing case, first slacken the front crankshaft pulley bolt. Bend back the locking tab and then, using a fabricated small piece of flywheel ring gear or a large pry bar, lock the engine and unscrew the bolt. The pulley can now be gently tapped off the end of the crankshaft.

4.79. Remove all the bolts and nuts that are securing the timing case – make sure to note their positions due to different lengths – then break the gasket seal and remove the cover. Lift out the governor plate and inspect for wear and scoring; if found, the part should be replaced as it could cause problems with the operation of the governor as well as problems with engine response.

4.80. If the camshaft sprocket is to be removed, note the pop marks which enable the timing of the valves to be maintained. The governor weights are

attached to the sprocket and these can be replaced if found to be worn or jamming with the governor plate.

4.81. If the timing chain is the original part then it will not have a joiner and, therefore, the cam sprocket will need to be removed along with the chain. Later timing chains and replacement types use a joining link. As the chain has no tensioner, any wear to the chain will cause poor running due to valve and ignition wander so it is imperative that you always replace the chain on overhaul.

4.82. Unbolt the rear camshaft plate from the block and then remove the eight cam followers, keeping them in order. The camshaft can then be rotated and withdrawn from the engine.

4.83. To remove the pistons, bend back the locking tabs for each connecting rod bolt. These must be replaced with new parts upon refitting the pistons.

4.85. Con rod numbers

4.84. Remove the big end bearing cap and, using a piece of wooden dowel, push out each piston in turn and refit the respective caps.

4.85. Each connecting rod is numbered to ensure the piston can be refitted to its relevant cylinder if being reused. This also helps to guarantee that the two halves of the caps match. (Number four con rod shown.)

4.86. Remove flywheel

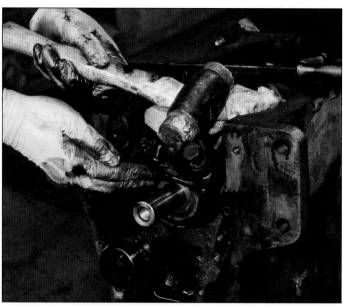

4.87. Tap out main bearing caps

4.88. Rear seal cover

4.89. Lift out crank

4.86. Bend back each flywheel bolt lock tab and remove the bolts. The next step is to lever off the flywheel, noting its locating dowel. (Take care as the unit is very heavy.) The rear crankshaft oil seal is leaking as shown by the black engine oil stain on the crankshaft.

4.87. Remove the back plate for the timing case, noting the position and number of brass washers fitted to the crankshaft. Bend back the main bearing lock tabs and undo the bolt. Using the bolts as levers, gently tap out the bearing caps from the block.

4.88. To replace the rear seal and/or remove the crankshaft, first remove the two round plates locating the rear oil seal.

The oil seal can then be lifted out from the rear of the crankshaft.

4.89. With the main and big end bearing caps removed, the crankshaft can now be lifted out of the engine block.

4.90. The dark lines on the crankshaft indicate wear and slight scoring is evident on the surface of the journals. This will require the crankshaft to be reground before new oversized shell bearings are fitted and the crankshaft is reinstalled into the engine. (See page 38 for other crankshaft faults.)

4.91. A Mercia gauge can be used to quickly assess the bore not only for wear (ridges) but – just as important – for ovality (out of roundness) and taper. If this is not checked, then new

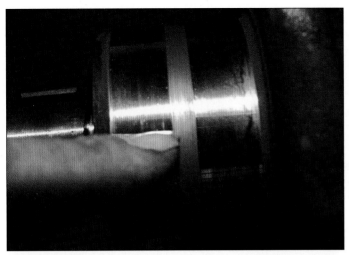

4.90. Crank wear

4.91. Measure bore wear

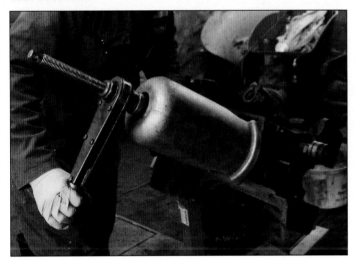

4.92. Remove liner

4.93. Remove exhaust manifold

rings will be unable to seal effectively in the cylinder bore. Therefore, to ensure a reliable engine, new liners should be fitted.

4.92. The cylinder liners on the 4-cylinder (87 mm) engine are located in the engine block by the cylinder head. This means that if the head is removed and the engine is turned the liner could lift up and lose its lower sealing or allow the bottom piston ring to drop out. To avoid this you should always fit washer/tubes on second and fourth head studs on the manifold side. This means that the engine can be overhauled without the necessity of a re-bore. A liner puller (or hydraulic press) is sometimes required to force the old liners out of the block if corrosion has occurred.

4.93. When removing the inlet/exhaust manifold make sure to note the locations of the long bolts for attachment of the heat shield for the TVO engine. Always renew the manifold gasket when reassembling.

4.94. If the valves need to be removed, for safety a special valve spring compressor tool should be used. This also makes it easy to remove and refit the valves. Make sure the parts are kept in order to enable a closer inspection and so you know where they belong in the engine. Use a copper hammer to break the taper collet's grip on the valve tips.

If the valves have excessive sideways movement in the cylinder head, then the valve guides need to be replaced. They cannot be punched out as this will damage the guides. A mandrel machined to fit the guide is required and also a hydraulic press to remove and refit them. The protrusion from the spring seat surface to the top of the valve guide measures 14.3 mm (9/16 in) for both inlets and exhausts.

4.94. Remove valves

4.95. The valve faces and seats can then be inspected for wear. The valve in the picture shows typical face recession due to prolonged operation. All the valves will either need to be replaced or the faces re-cut. The seats in the cylinder head will have the same damage and they too will need to be re-cut.

4.96. The valve faces are re-cut to 45 degree angles using a special tungsten cutter. This ensures a narrow width seat for the valve face and achieves excellent sealing. Alternatively, a local engine reconditioner can carry out the work.

4.97. This is the new surface – smooth and parallel – after using the valve face cutter.

4.98. As the springs age, they will stretch; therefore, to check their condition you should measure the free spring length. This should not exceed 43.6 mm (1.716 in). Always replace springs in sets.

4.99. The valve seats are cut to a 15 degree top angle, a 45 degree seat angle and a 60 degree bottom angle using a special tungsten cutter. This ensures a narrow width seat for the

4.95. Valve face depression

4.96. Cut valve face

4.97. Cut face

valve face and achieves excellent sealing. Alternatively, a local engine reconditioner can carry out the work.

4.100. Using fine grinding paste and a suction stick the valve seat and face

4.98. Valve spring length

4.99. Cut valve seats

4.100. Lap in valves

4.101. Rocker tips wear

4.102. Refit valve collets

4.103. Level oil pump end plate

are matched together by rotating the stick and applying a downward force. When a faint grey line appears on both surfaces the sealing can be checked – after fitting the valve springs, etc. – by filling the ports with diesel or paraffin and looking for leaks. If these are evident, then further grinding will be necessary.

4.101. If you do not regularly adjust the valve tip clearance it can result in a gap that is too large. This hammers the rocker and consequently causes rapid wear as shown by the depression on the tip. Either replace with good second-hand rockers or carefully grind level. (As shown by the rocker tips in the picture.)

4.102. The valve components can be replaced with a valve spring compressor. A small amount of grease will hold the small collets in place and make the process easier.

4.103. One area often overlooked when inspecting an engine is the engine oil pump, specifically the internals. If the engine is found to be worn, then it is likely that the internals of the engine oil pump will be past their best; this can result in low oil flow and pressure within the lubrication

4.104. Oil pump parts

system of the engine. Any scoring or marks will necessitate the replacement of the pump. Check the operating clearance between the peaks of the inner and outer rotors using a feeler gauge. The limit is 0.1524 mm (0.006 in). Clearance between the outer rotor and the pump housing has a limit of 0.254 mm (0.010 in) and this should also be checked. Finally, using a straight edge, check that the gap between the top of the rotors and the pump body does not exceed 0.101 mm (0.004 in). To smooth out marks, use a 360 wet and dry emery paper on a glass (flat) surface.

4.104. The inner and outer rotor parts are available and should be fitted when overhauling the engine, or if low oil pressure is evident – typical oil pressure when hot should be 40 to 60 psi. Before fitting the rotor parts you should first check that the oil filter or the sump gauze strainer is not blocked.

4.105. Bore to piston clearance

4.106. Piston ring groove

4.107. Fit new pistons

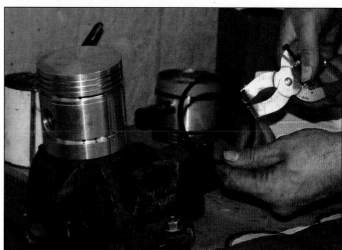

4.108. Fit piston and rings

4.105. If oil consumption has increased or there is a pronounced wear ridge at the top of the bore, then the liner should be replaced. To assess if the piston can be reused, the clearance between the piston skirt and the bore should be measured with a feeler gauge. If it exceeds 0.178 mm (0.007 in), then the cylinder liner and piston will need to be replaced.

4.106. Remove the old piston rings and use a feeler gauge to check the piston ring groove width. The range is described in the adjacent table. If the widths exceed the measurements given then the piston must be replaced as the ring could move in the groove and snap, causing extensive engine damage.

Ring	Width
Top and 2nd ring	2.558 mm (0.100 in)
3rd ring	4.930 mm (0.194 in)
4th ring	4.130 mm (0.163 in)

4.109. Stagger ring gaps

4.110. Fit pistons to bore

4.111. Torque big end caps

4.107. The pistons were found to be worn so new ones will need to be fitted. To remove the old piston, lift out the circlips and slide out the gudgeon pin. Note the position of the piston split skirt in relation to the numbers on the connecting rod; then refit with the gudgeon pin supplied with each piston. Fit new circlips. Check the small end bush movement in the new gudgeon pin; any appreciable play will necessitate fitting new bushes. The final step is to ream to fit but this work will probably need to be done by a machine shop.

4.108. The new piston rings are supplied in sets and are packaged to ensure the correct position on the piston. Note some rings have to be fitted with the word 'TOP' facing the piston crown because of the shape of the ring face. Always use a piston ring expander to prevent breakages.

4.109. With all the rings fitted, stagger the rings so that the gaps are 180 degrees apart.

4.110. Apply copious amounts of clean engine oil and fit the piston ring compressor. When fitting to the engine, lubricate the engine bore and crank journal, then gently tap into the respective bores (as marked on the con rod end).

4.111. Lubricate the new big end shell bearings while noting the small notch which locates the bearing in the con rod. This also aligns the oil feed hole to the small end bush to lubricate the gudgeon pin. Fit new locking tabs and tighten the con rod bolts to between 69 and 76 Nm (50 and 55 lb-ft).

4.112. Finally bend over the lock tabs with a pair of pipe grip pliers.

4.113. Ensure that the liner seal surface in the block is scrupulously clean and free from dirt, corrosion and oil; this will enable it to seal fully to prevent coolant entering the oil in the sump. Then fit new cylinder sleeves by tapping down gently with a copper hammer until slightly proud of the gasket surface on the block.

4.112. Bend lock tab pistons

4.113. Fit liner seal

4.114. Measure liner stand out

4.116. Torque main bearings

4.114. To ensure that the head gasket seals correctly and also to provide the force to seal to the lower liner, both parts must protrude above the engine block by 0.076 to 0.018 mm (0.003 to 0.0007 in) when initially fitted. Note that the flat edges of the liners face each other.

4.115. In this case the crankshaft has been reground before fitting. Make sure to clean the crankshaft to remove any metal left from the machining process and blow out the oil ways. Oversized big end and main shell bearings are matched to the amount machined off the journals. The main shell bearings are located by the notches, used to align oilways, in their respective housings. Fit the engine block main shell bearings and lubricate with clean engine oil. Then fit the rear oil seal to the crankshaft (with the lip of the seal facing inwards) and lower the crank into the block.

4.116. When fitting the individual main bearing caps you should torque the bolts to 117.52 to 124.43 Nm (85 to 90 lb-ft) and then rotate the engine to ensure smooth operation. If the engine binds or will not turn, you will need to remove the cap and recheck for faults.

4.115. Main bearing fit

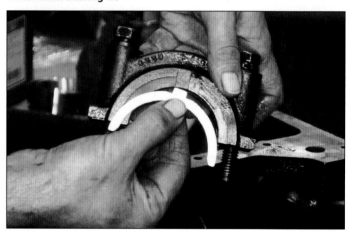

4.117. Thrust bearing

4.118. Main cap and rear seal

4.119. Gasket to seal front block

4.120. Fit seals to end bearing

4.117. Place the four thrust washers with the oil grooves facing outwards onto the centre housings using grease.

4.118. The rear main bearing cap has rear wick seal grooves. Apply gasket sealer to the grooves, then fit the cap and ensure it is flush with the end of the block. Push the rear crank seal in so it is level with the rear surface of the block.

4.119. The front main bearing has a bridge piece for the sump to press against. Fit the cork seal to the ends and tap the bridge into position. Secure with the two cheese-headed screws.

4.120. Lubricate the two wick seals with gasket sealer and then fit them to the rear main bearing cap and push the seals down into the groove until completely filled using a thin piece of (welding) wire.

4.121. After overhauling the engine internals, fitting a new oil pump and cleaning the sump of sludge, you can then fit a new sump gasket with sealer and lower it onto the block. Fit all the bolts and then torque to the correct setting. Apply sealer to the new gasket and fit the oil pump gauze filter into the sump. It is important not to over tighten the nuts as this will distort the thin housing and cause an oil leak.

4.122. Clean the front of the block and fit a new gasket with sealer. Align the rear timing plate holes and fit securing bolts.

4.123. Lubricate and refit the camshaft, cam followers and governor weights and plate.

4.121. Fitting sump

4.122. Timing gasket and plate

4.123. Governor plate

4.124. Timing marks

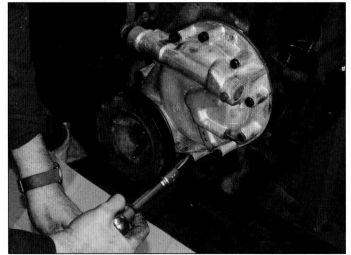

4.125. Timing chain clip

4.126. Timing case and spacers

4.127. Timing cover fit

4.124. To check the cam and distributor timing, first ensure that the pop marks on the cam and cam sprocket are still visible. Fit the crankshaft sprocket making sure that the brass shims are fitted first to ensure that the two sprockets are in line. Rotate the engine until number one cylinder is at Top Dead Centre (TDC), i.e. the top of its movement in the bore. The two (faint) timing marks should now face each other as shown.

4.125. Fit the timing chain and slide the joiner through the links, fit the side link and the 'C' retaining clip. The open end should be facing away from the direction of rotation.

4.126. Before refitting the timing case you should fit a new crankshaft oil seal to the casing and to the brass spacers and large washer. This large washer is otherwise known as an oil flinger; it reduces the oil load in the seal.

4.127. Refit the timing cover with a new gasket. Fit all the nuts and bolts loosely and then slide on the front crank pulley; this will align the front seal. The bolts can then be tightened to the correct torque.

4.128. The long shaft provides the drive for the engine oil pump as well as the distributor. A very small woodruff key locks it into the drive gear from the camshaft. It is very

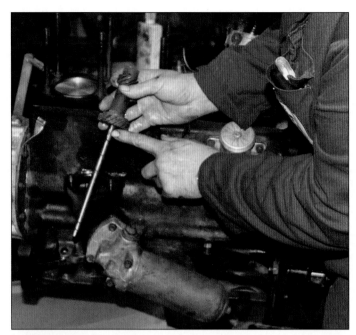

4.128. Drive key for distributor and oil pump

4.129. Position of slot for distributor

4.130. Distributor drive plate

4.131. Distributor rotor arm position

important that this is fitted, otherwise the engine will not have any lubricating oil pressure.

4.129. The distributor is driven from the camshaft and must be timed with the number one cylinder to produce a spark in the compression stroke. To ensure the timing is correct when fitting the drive gear, the number one piston must be at 10 degrees before the top of its compression stroke. At this time both valves will be closed. This can be determined by rotating the engine with all the plugs removed except number one. Turn the engine over by hand until compression resistance is felt.

On the left-hand side of the engine is a 6 mm hole. Slide a bar in and at the same time turn the engine, the bar

will pop into the hole in the flywheel at the correct piston position. The drive gear can now be fitted at a 45 degree angle as shown.

4.130. With a new gasket, fit the distributor and engine tachometer drive plate.

4.131. Do not turn the engine from the position shown in picture 4.129 above. The distributor should now fit onto its drive plate in one position only as the slot in the drive gear is offset. The rotor arm should face the number one cylinder mark (white blob) in the periphery of the body. Do not fully tighten the distributor clamp as slight running adjustment will be necessary.

4.132. Fit head and gasket

4.132. Clean the head and engine block gasket surfaces of oil, etc. and then fit the new head gasket. Take note of the 'TOP' mark on one side of the gasket: this should face upwards. Do not apply any gasket sealer to the gasket as it is pre-fitted with a layer of special sealer.

4.133. Gently lower the cylinder head onto the engine block and fit all the nuts with the relevant washers and the heat shield. Tighten the nuts in the sequence shown in three stages up to a final figure between 82.95 and 89.87 Nm (60–65 lb-ft).

4.134. Locate the push rods into their respective cam followers and fit the caps to the top of the valve stems. Fit the pedestal nuts and washer and tighten evenly to the set torque, ensuring that the push rods locate in the rocker arms.

4.133. Head torque order

4.134. Fit push rods and valve tip caps

4.135. Check valve clearances

4.136. Fit rocker cover

4.137. Flywheel timing marks

4.135. Set the valve clearance using the Rule of Nine procedure (page 50) with the gaps adjusted to inlet valves 0.254 mm (0.010 in) and exhaust valves 0.304 mm (0.012 in) respectively. Turn the engine over slowly by turning fan blade by hand; alternatively, use the starting handle with the battery disconnected to prevent the engine from running.

Watch the valves of one cylinder open and the opposite cylinder (i.e. one and four) close in unison with each other, e.g. one valve opening (rocker moving down) and one closing (rocker moving up). Set the valve clearances of the corresponding valves as shown on page 50.

4.136. Before fitting the rocker cover. Glue the cork gasket to the cleaned metal cover and then when cured, fit the rocker cover to the engine dry. This will allow the cover to be removed easily when you want to check cylinder head tightness and valve clearances after 25–30 hours of work.

4.137. Timing marks are visible on the flywheel to assist with camshaft and ignition timing. These can be viewed through the starter motor hole.

MF 35 3-cylinder 3.152 Engine Overhaul
This 3-cylinder engine was developed by Perkins engines of Peterborough and directly replaced the 4-cylinder 23c diesel engine in 1959.

Data Specifications

Cylinders	3
Bore	91.44 mm (3.6 in)
Stroke	5 in
Displacement	152.7 cu ins.
Compression Ratio	17.4:1
Firing Order	1,2,3
Power	37 bhp
Location of No. 1 Cylinder	Front of engine
Cylinder Liners	Chrome plated
Fuel Pump Static Timing	18 degrees B.T.D.C.
Letter On Fuel Pump Rotor	E
Letter on Hydraulic Head No. 1 Delivery Port	W
Inlet Valve Opens	13 degrees B.T.D.C.
Exhaust Valve Closes	10 degrees A.T.D.C.
Valve Overlap Valve Lift Tappet Setting (Hot)	23 degrees 0.36 in 0.25 mm (0.010 in)
Tappet Setting (Cold)	0.30 mm (0.012 in)
Pressure Setting (injector bleeding pressure)	120 bar
Operating Oil Pressure	25–30 psi or more at normal speed
Relief Valve Setting	50–65 psi

TIGHTENING TORQUES

	Nm	lb-ft
Cylinder Head Nuts	81 Nm	55 – 60
Con. Rod Nuts	95 Nm	70 – 80
Main Bearing Setscrews	150 Nm	110 – 120
Flywheel Setscrews	105 Nm	75
Balance Weight Setscrews	75 Nm	50 – 55

The pictures demonstrate the areas of wear typically found in an old, worn-out engine as well as the tasks you will have to perform in order to restore the engine to a good working order.

4.138. Engine blow by

4.138. If oil splashes out of the tube when you remove the engine oil dipstick, then the engine piston rings and bore are probably worn out together with the rest of the internal engine parts, such as the shell bearings and crankshaft. Check first that the engine breather is not blocked as this can give the same effect.

4.139. With the engine removed from the tractor, one indication of internal wear is the fore and aft movement of the crankshaft. Excessive play relates to worn thrust washers and usually other worn-out engine parts.

4.140. With the bonnet and fuel tank removed, the tractor can be split at the transmission bell housing. This will enable easier access to the engine and gearbox for disassembly and closer inspection. Conveniently, the engine is fitted with lifting eyes that permit lifting straps and a crane or overhead gantry to remove the front of the tractor.

4.139. Excessive crank shaft end float

4.140. Engine separated

4.141. Remove rocker cover and fuel pipes

4.142. Remove rocker shaft

4.143. Remove head

4.141. Remove the external fuel pipes to enable the engine internal components to be extracted. Make sure to note their positions with labelling. Then remove the rocker cover.

4.142. Unbolt the small oil feed pipe on the right-hand rear of the cylinder head and then remove the rocker, retaining the nuts evenly.

4.143. To remove the cylinder head, slacken the head nuts and bolts in the order of tightening (see picture on page 78). Then gently tap the edge of the head with a copper hammer to release the stuck gasket. Do not wedge anything in between the head and the block as this will damage the gasket surface.

4.144. Head gasket blown

4.145. Lift off sump

4.146. Sump wick housing

4.147. Remove oil pump

4.144. The head gasket has not been sealing between number one and two engine cylinders. This will lead to a loss of pressure within the bores and is one of the factors contributing to the engine's poor starting and performance.

4.145. Remove the short bolts and the nuts hidden inside the sump recess at the rear. Lift the engine off the sump; it may need tapping with a copper hammer to break the gasket seal.

4.146. The small aluminium half moon housing can now be unbolted from the bottom of the engine block. This allows a cork gasket to seal the front edge of the sump to the engine block.

4.147. The small drive gear to the oil pump can be removed by sliding off the 'C' clip. With a very thin spanner remove the three bolts that hold the pump to the front main bearing cap. At the same time, the oil feed pipes should be loosened and twisted away when the pump is taken off.

4.148. One area often overlooked when inspecting an engine is the internals of the engine oil pump. This will be past its best if the engine is also found to be worn, resulting in low oil flow and pressure within the lubrication system of the engine. Any scoring or marks will necessitate the replacement of the pump. Check the operating clearance using a feeler gauge between the peaks

4.148. Oil pump wear

4.149. Remove pistons

4.150. Piston damage

4.151. Remove rings

of the inner and outer rotors. The limit is 0.1524 mm (0.006 in). Clearance between the outer rotor and the pump housing limit is 0.254 mm (0.010 in). Use a straight edge to check that the gap between the top of the rotors and the pump body does not exceed 0.0762 mm (0.003 in).

4.149. Rotate the engine until the piston to be removed is at the bottom of the block. Slacken the two big end bearing caps and then remove the cap, shell

bearing and bolts. Turn the engine to push the piston to the top and, using a wooden dowel, push the piston out of the bore. Refit the relevant cap and bolts and repeat with the other pistons.

4.150. After our initial testing we had expected to see poor piston and bore condition, but instead the 'lands' between the top compression piston rings on number two and

three cylinders have broken up and disintegrated. This has led to snapped piston rings and caused the rings to lose their ability to seal effectively.

4.151. Using the correct expanding tool remove the piston rings to assess for wear and check the piston ring grooves for the correct gap. If reusing the rings ensure you keep them in the correct position and order. When refitting make sure to match the ring grooves and the bore wear.

4.152. Ring groove wear

4.152. Using a feeler gauge check the piston ring groove. The table describes the acceptable range of measurements.

Ring groove width	
Top and 2nd ring	2.43/2.46 mm (0.0957/0.0967 in)
3rd ring	3.23/3.25 mm (0.127/0.128 in)
4th and 5th ring	6.40/6.43 mm (0.252/0.253 in)

If the gaps exceed these measurements then the piston must be replaced because the ring can move in the groove and possibly snap, causing extensive engine damage.

4.153. Some engines use the laminated ring sets in the lower grooves. This improves sealing and reduces oil loss. **(Refer to the instruction leaflet that is supplied with the rings.)**

Laminated compression rings

The laminated compression ring fitted in the third groove is different on early and later engines.

On early engines, it consisted of three segments. On later engines, it consisted of four segments.

It is important that the laminated compression ring is correctly assembled to the piston.

4.153. Flex rings position

4.154. After conducting a compression test with the cylinder head removed it becomes clear that all is not well with the engine's internals. The ridge at the top of the bore is quite pronounced. This indicates excessive wear of the cylinder liner which has resulted in loss of piston ring sealing: another cause of poor starting. Maximum wear is 0.18 mm (0.007 in).

4.155. With the piston ring removed and the top of the bore cleaned, the piston ring end gap can be checked. This will give an indication of how worn the piston rings are and whether they can be reused. Experience suggests that they should be replaced as a matter of course.

Maximum permissible measurements for the piston ring end gap		
Ring gap	Top	0.36/0.76 mm (0.014/0.030 in)
Ring gap	2nd and scraper	0.28/0.69 mm (0.011/0.027 in)

4.156. Using a Mercia gauge the bore can be quickly assessed not only for wear (ridge) but also for ovality (out of roundness) and taper. If not checked/determined it will cause new rings to be unable to seal effectively in the cylinder bore. Therefore new liners should be fitted to ensure a reliable engine.

4.154. Bore wear ridge

4.155. Check piston ring end gap

4.156. Bore wear Mercia gauge

4.157. Liner sleeve removal

4.158. Rear crank seal

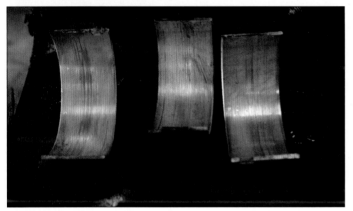

4.159. Big end shell scoring

4.160. Main shell bearing worn

4.157. The cylinder liners on the 3-cylinder engines are an interference press fit into the engine block. This means that the engine can be overhauled without the necessity of a re-bore. A hydraulic press will be required to force the old liners out of the bore and push the new liners in.

4.158 To remove the rear crankshaft seal housing, first disconnect the two nuts and bolts securing the two halves together. Then remove the six retaining bolts making sure to note the thin heads of the special bolts.

4.159. Lack of oil pressure, worn crankshaft and poor fitting has caused these new shell bearings to score the soft white metal bearing surface.

4.160. These are the original main shell bearings: the white metal has, over time, simply worn away. This leads to low engine oil pressure and rapid wear of the crankshaft. Note the crescent-shaped washers, which control the end float of thrust of the crankshaft fore and aft. These washers should be replaced when overhauling the engine.

4.161. The dark lines on the crankshaft indicate wear. Also, there is evidence of slight scoring on the surface of the

4.161. Worn old crank

journals. This will require the crankshaft to be reground before new shell bearings are fitted and the crankshaft reinstalled in the engine. To remove the crankshaft the engine will need to be unbolted from the tractor. Then the sump, oil pump, timing case, connecting rods and main bearing caps will need to be

4.162. Crankshaft regrind

disconnected. Before removing the two counterweights, their relative positions need to be marked to ensure that they are refitted in the correct orientation to maintain balance.

4.162. To remove scoring, out of roundness and blemishes on the crankshaft journal surfaces, a special lathe/grinder is utilised which produces a perfectly round and smooth mirror finish. New shell bearings (which are not normally included in an engine overhaul kit) will be required and are available in three different thicknesses depending upon the amount of metal that had to be ground off the bearing journals to make them good. These should be ordered after the regrind.

4.163. To prevent the valve contacting the pistons and to maintain a good

cylinder compression it is important to maintain the valve face depth below the cylinder head. The maximum permissible valve head depth in service for the 3.152 engine is 3.50 mm (0.140 in). If the valves exceed this figure then either new valves and/or new seats will need to be fitted.

4.164. If the valves need to be removed, then a special valve spring compressor tool should be used for the sake of safety. This enables you to remove and fit the valves easily. Make sure to take note of the position of the parts within the engine. It is also advisable to keep the parts in order so that you can have a closer inspection.

4.165. The valve faces and seats can then be inspected for wear. The two valves in the picture show typical face recession and damage meaning that they will either need to be replaced or the faces

4.163. Valve face depth

re-cut. The seats in the cylinder head will have the same damage so they too will need to be refaced. Alternatively, you could fit a new cylinder head.

4.166. As the springs age, they will stretch, so it is important to check the condition. Measure the free spring length. Note: in some engines two springs are fitted to give the required force to seal the valves. Springs are available in sets and should all be replaced together.

4.164. Remove valves

4.165. Worn valve faces

Outer valve springs	
Free length	42.29/45.80 mm (1.783/1.803 in)
Fitted length	38.10 mm (1.500 in)
Load at fitted length	10.34 kg ± 0.90 kg (22.75 lb ± 2 lb)
Inner valve springs (where fitted)	
Free length	34.67/35.69 mm (1.365/1.405 in)
Fitted length	30.16 mm (1.1875 in)
Load at fitted length	3.63 kg ± 0.45 kg (8.0 lb ± 1 lb)

4.167. Using a special tungsten cutter, the valve seats are cut to a 15 degree top angle, a 45 degree seat angle and a 60 degree bottom angle. This ensures a narrow width seat for the valve face and achieves excellent sealing. Alternatively, a local engine reconditioner could carry out the work for you.

4.168. This is the layout of the valve train. Note the washer at the bottom of the spring; this locates the spring and prevents it from wearing the cylinder head.

4.169. In order for the head gasket to properly seal, the faces of the block and cylinder head must be completely clean of dirt and carbon. Use wet and dry emery paper on a block of hard wood to achieve a good finish. A machined straight edge is used to

4.166. Valve spring height

4.167. Valve seat cutter

4.168. Valve train layout

4.169. Cylinder head flatness

check the cylinder head surface flatness with a feeler gauge. End to end distortion measuring 0.15 mm (0.006 in) and side to side distortion measuring 0.08 mm (0.003 in) is required before machining. The straight edge can also be utilised to check the valve face below the head surface.

4.170. The aluminium timing case is fitted to the engine block. Ensure the idler gear hub is fitted in the correct position by using the locating dowel and the pin. They should align the hub correctly, which will allow for oil lubrication.

4.170. Fitting old timing case

4.171. Camshaft fitting

4.172. Torque main caps

4.173. Refit pistons

4.173a. Ring gaps not staggered

4.171. To remove the camshaft, the timing cover is first lifted off the engine. Then the camshaft can be withdrawn provided the cylinder head and fuel lift pump have already been removed. Inspect the cam lobes for wear and scoring and replace if in any doubt. Lubricate with clean engine oil.

4.172. Using grease to hold in place fit the crankshaft thrust washers to the rear bearing housing. Place the new main bearing shells in their respective housings with the tab locating them. Apply clean engine oil and then fit the new shells to the caps and slide into place in their respective (numbered) positions. Torque each bearing cap to 150 Nm (110–120 lb-ft), turning the engine over one revolution to ensure all is correct and free moving. Finally bend over the lock tabs to prevent the bolt unscrewing.

4.173. & 4.173a. Once all the rings have been fitted, stagger the rings so that the gaps are 180 degrees apart. Apply copious amounts of clean engine oil and fit the piston ring compressor. When fitting to the engine, lubricate the engine bore and crank journal (with clean engine oil). Then gently tap the pistons into their respective bores (as marked on con rod end).

4.174. Wick rear crank seal

4.175. Rear crank seals

It is important to fit new con rod nuts – do not use the old ones! – and torque to 95 Nm (80 lb-ft). Finally, bend over the lock tabs and rotate the engine one revolution to ensure all is ok.

4.174. Two types of rear crankshaft seals are fitted to the 3-cylinder Massey Ferguson (Perkins) engine. The early type is a wick or rope type and the later model uses a modern rubber lip seal. When purchasing a crankshaft ensure you order the correct type for your engine's age.

4.175. To fit the early wick or rope type rear seals to the housings, first immerse in clean engine oil for at least 1 hour. Then fit the seals as follows:

1. Put one half housing in a vice with the seal recess to the top.

2. Fit 25 mm (1 in) of the seal at each end into the ends of the groove so that each end of the seal extends 0.25/0.50 mm (0.010/0.020 in) above the half housing end face.

3. Press the remainder of the seal into the groove by hand. Start this operation from the centre of the seal. Then use a round shaft to roll in the seal by the use of pressure on its inside diameter.

4. Fit seal to other half housing as already indicated.

4.176. 3-cylinder timing marks

5. Clean the half housing faces.

6. Lightly apply jointing compound to both sides of the joint and put the joint in position.

7. Lightly apply jointing compound to the end faces of the half housings.

8. Make sure to tighten the set screw and nuts to 16 Nm (12 lb-ft).

4.176. The timing gears in the engine are connected by a central idler gear and the timing marks will only align in one position due to their offsets. Position the marks on the camshaft, injection pump and crankshaft gear to face each other and then fit the idler gear. Tighten the bolt to 68 Nm (50 lb-ft) and bend the lock tab over to secure.

4.177. Clean the head and engine block gasket surfaces and then fit the new head gasket, taking note of the 'TOP' mark. Do not apply any gasket sealer to the gasket as it is pre-fitted with a layer of special sealer.

4.177. Fitting cylinder head

4.178. Head bolt layout

4.178. Gently lower the cylinder head onto the engine block. Fit all the bolts and nuts with flat washers and tighten the bolts in the sequence shown in three stages up to a final figure 81 Nm (60 lb-ft). After you have run the engine for 25 to 50 hours it is important to remember to re-torque the head bolts and nuts.

4.179. Adjust the valve clearances so that both the inlet and exhaust valves are set to 0.30 mm (0.012 in) with the engine cold.

First turn the engine over in the normal direction or rotation until the number one cylinder (front of the engine) inlet valve has opened and the exhaust valve of the same cylinder has just closed. Then check and adjust the clearance of the number four and six valves with a feeler gauge.

Mark the front pulley and timing case and then rotate the engine one revolution (360 degrees) until the marks realign again and check and adjust the clearances of the number one, two, three and five valves.

If the valve clearances require adjusting, three spanners will be needed to lengthen or shorten the cam follower. It is easier to carry out the task with two people.

4.179. Set valve clearances

4.180. With all the ancillaries – water pump, fuel injection pump, dynamo, flywheel and clutch – fitted, the engine is ready to be bolted back onto the tractor. Before starting the engine, fill with clean engine oil and ideally fit an accurate oil pressure gauge. (If necessary use the dash-mounted one.) Crank the engine over until the oil pressure has registered: only then will you be able to bleed the fuel system and run up the engine.

4.180. New engine ready to fit

Chapter 5 Cooling Systems

Inside your tractor's engine, controlled explosions are caused by igniting the fuel/air mixture. These explosions are converted into power that drives the PTO and wheels but in doing so they produce a large amount of heat (up to 2,000 °Celsius). These high temperatures are controlled with the help of the forced circulation liquid cooling system.

Your vehicle's cooling system is a crucial part of the engine and maintaining it properly will make the engine last longer and perform better. However, the engine must not be overcooled and an ideal operating coolant temperature is between 80° and 94 °Celsius. When the engine is cold, the thermostat is closed and the coolant is circulated around the engine block by the water pump via the bypass hose. This enables the temperature of the coolant to rise quickly and reach the correct operating temperature.

About 33% of fuel is converted into actual power, and about 67% is converted into heat. A cooling system protects an engine from damage by transferring this heat to the atmosphere through the radiator. The correct operating temperature is a critical part of the proper functioning of the engine. The thermostat opens at 82° to 94 °Celsius and coolant is then allowed to flow with the assistance of the water pump into the radiator. It then flows back into the engine via the bottom hose.

Engine coolant is used to transfer heat from the engine operation via the top hose to the radiator by the cooling passages within the engine block. The radiator removes heat from the coolant by forcing cooler air through the radiator fins with the aid of a fan.

The water pump pushes heated coolant from inside the engine block, past the thermostat to the top of the radiator, then the liquid flows down though the tubes. The fan, which is driven by a belt via the crankshaft, draws cool air through the radiator fins to help speed cooling. The coolant is then forced through the bottom hose and pumped back into the engine block. When the engine is cold the thermostat blocks off the passage to the top of the radiator until the coolant reaches between 82° and 94 °Celsius.

Tractors from the early 1930s and '40s did not have radiator pressure caps and would have to have their coolant systems topped up three to four times a day. Later tractors incorporated a pressurised cap that would seal the coolant into the system and enable it to work at a high operating temperature (82° to 94 °Celsius) without the risk of losses due to vaporisation or boiling of the coolant. The cap pressurises and seals the system to between 0.28 and 0.90 bar (4 and 13 psi) depending upon the engine fitted.

Without coolant the engine will overheat and if left unattended severe engine damage will occur. An improperly maintained cooling system can result in the overheating of the engine, which in turn can cause major component seizures within.

Tools required for checks:

Range of imperial spanners and ⅜, ½ and ¾ drive socket sets

Flat and Philips blade screwdrivers

Hammer and small chisel

Valve stand tray

Trolley jack(s) and axle stands

Wooden wedges

Drain pans

Parts containers and masking tape

Protective gloves

Servicing the Cooling System

THERMOSTAT DATA

87 mm PETROL ENGINE
(Up to Engine Serial No. SG 5983E)

Valve opens	75-80°C	(167-176°F)
Valve fully open	95°C	(203°F)
Valve lift	.312 in	(7.93 mm)

(From Engine Serial No. SG 5984E)

Valve opens	76-81°C	(169°F-178°F)
Valve fully open	95°C	(203°F)
Valve lift	.312 in	(7.93 mm)

87 mm V.O. ENGINE
(Up to Engine Serial No. SH 406E)

Valve opens	75-80°C	(167-176°F)
Valve fully open	95°C	(203°F)
Valve lift	.312 in	(7.93 mm)

(From Engine Serial No. SH 407E)

Valve opens	76-81°C	(169-178°F)
Valve fully open	95°C	(203°F)

23C DIESEL ENGINE

Valve opens	68-73°C	(154-163°F)
Valve fully oper	85°C	(185°F)
Valve lift	.312 in	(7.94 mm)

3-A-152 DIESEL ENGINE

Valve opens	80°C	(176°F)
Valve fully open	93°C	(199°F)
Valve lift	.34 in	(8.65 mm)

To ensure efficient running of the engine and to prevent wear the thermostat for the various engines must operate at the correct temperatures as shown.

5.01. 3-cylinder cooling system layout

5.01. Layout of the parts and names for the 3-cylinder 3.152 diesel engine.

5.01a. Layout of the parts and names for the 4-cylinder 23c diesel engine.

5.02. When servicing the tractor, it is worth checking the strength of the antifreeze and if necessary adding more to the cooling system. A 50% mixture would give corrosion protection and freezing protection down to -30 °Celsius. If the liquid is brown or discoloured it must be flushed out and replaced with clean water and antifreeze. Depending upon the age of the tractor it may use monoethylene glycol-based antifreeze, which is usually blue in colour. The more modern systems use organic acid-based antifreeze which is green or pink in colour and is more environmentally friendly. Although this later type (which can be used safely in older systems) is more expensive, it has an operational life of five years as opposed to the 'blue' antifreeze which only lasts two to three years.

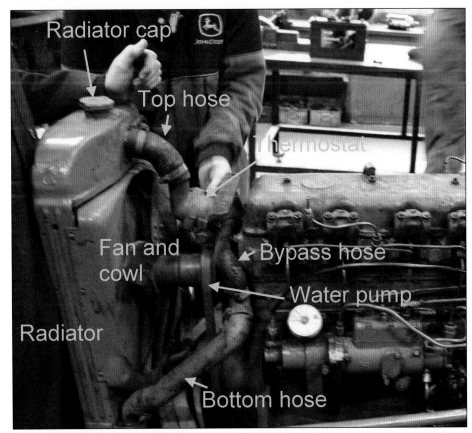

5.01a. 4-cylinder cooling system layout

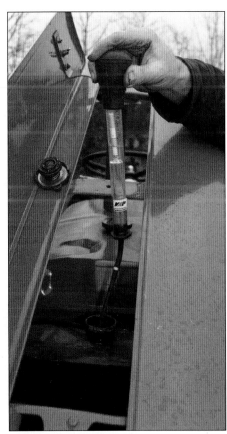

5.02. Check antifreeze

5.03. Engine internal corrosion

5.06. Pressure test

5.04. Rusted core plug

5.05. Split fan belt

5.03. This tractor's (MF 35 petrol/TVO) cylinder liners were removed to fit new ones because of excessive bore wear. As you can see extreme corrosion has taken place between the bores blocking the coolant passages and resulting in poor cooling of the engine. Never run an engine with just water in the cooling system as corrosion will occur.

5.04. If there is no antifreeze in the engine coolant that means the anti-corrosion additive is not protecting the bare metal internals of the system.

Unfortunately the core plugs are the weakest point and will corrode. If one plug fails, then very soon they all will. Always use antifreeze all year round.

5.05. Slacken off the dynamo, remove the fan belt and check its condition. This one is showing signs of slipping and cracking. Correct tension is 19 mm (¾ in) for a dynamo belt.

5.06. A simple pressure test pump fitted to the top of the radiator will highlight any leaks from the radiator, hoses, water

pump, gaskets or engine block. The same can be achieved by running the engine until it reaches its full operating temperature; the drawback to this method is that the engine will be hot so sometimes the leaking coolant will evaporate and be difficult to see. Note the water escaping from the perished top hose.

5.07. This MF 35 petrol\TVO tractor had a leaking water pump seal which was discovered by running the engine. In order to replace the pump unit, first

5.07. Water pump leak

5.08. Damaged radiator core

5.09. Coolant leaks

5.10. Radiator pressure cap

drain the coolant (only water in this case) using the drain taps on the radiator and left-hand side of the engine block. Then remove the fan belt and all the hoses. Unscrew three nuts and spring washers which secure the pump to the front timing cover and carefully – so as not to damage the radiator core – extract the pump via the right-hand side of the engine.

5.08. The tractor fitted with this radiator was running too hot due to a blocked radiator core caused by grass and dirt build up. It was also losing coolant because of damage in the radiator core tubes. If the radiator was not damaged, then the outside core could be cleaned with compressed air or with water pressure from a hose pipe and mains.

The internal cores can be 'reverse flushed' to remove any rust or accumulation of dirt. This entails putting the water hose up inside the bottom radiator connection and allowing the water to flow in the opposite direction until it runs clear.

5.09. Before changing or adding antifreeze to the cooling system, it is worth checking for any leaks. If you have been constantly topping up in the summer, then a leak from a perished hose or loose connection may be the problem.

5.10. Radiator pressure caps need to be inspected carefully to ensure the rubber seal is not perished or split and also that the correct one is fitted. The operating pressure is usually marked on the top of the cap – in this case 0.48 bar (7 psi).

5.11. The thermostat is fitted inside the housing at the front top end of the engine. It controls the running temperature of the engine. Unfortunately

thermostats can stick closed, leading to overheating, or remain open, which causes the engine to run too cold. Occasionally, slow response to engine running temperature will cause cool operation. Any of these faults can be detrimental to the life of the engine. Do not run the engine for any length of time without a thermostat fitted as this leads to poor coolant circulation and overheating of the rear engine cylinders.

5.12. If you suspect that the thermostat is not working correctly – i.e. stuck open or closed or slow to operate – then remove the thermostat from the engine and immerse it in warm water. Then, with a thermometer in the water, heat slowly. Note the temperature that the valve starts to open: this is usually between 82° and 94 °Celsius. The temperature on the thermometer should correspond with the

5.11. Thermostat for 4-cylinder 23c

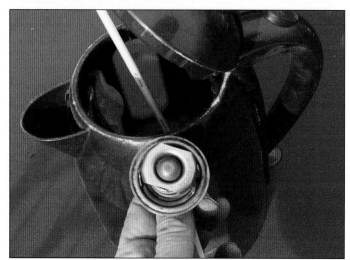

5.12. Test thermostat

5.13. Fit new thermostat for TVO engine

temperature marked on the thermostat. (It is 88 °Celsius in the picture.) If it is slow to open or fails to open then replace the unit.

5.13. When fitting a new thermostat make sure to fit it the right way around (see picture) to ensure that it works properly. Use a new gasket and sealant to prevent leaks.

5.14. To remove the radiator, first drain the coolant into a container and then slacken off the top and bottom radiator hoses. Slacken off the lower retaining nuts and lift off the front axle casing. (In the picture the work is being done on a 4-cylinder 23c engine.)

5.15. The procedure for removing the 4-cylinder petrol engine radiator is the same; however, if you are purchasing a new radiator it is worth noting that

there are three types used on Massey Ferguson 35 tractors, depending upon the engine fitted. The variations to each type concern the position and angle of the top pipe and the location of the top support tie rod.

5.16. Mark the front of the fan blades to ensure they are refitted in the correct orientation on reassembly; otherwise cooling problems could occur under heavy work. The same pump is used on both the 4-cylinder 23c and petrol/TVO 85 mm engines so the procedure is the same. To remove the front hub, first slacken the centre lock nut and then remove the lock nut and cotter pin: this will enable the hub to be pulled off the water pump spindle.

5.17. The water pump on the 4-cylinder 23c and the petrol/TVO 85 mm engines

is separate from the housing attached to the engine block. By grasping the fan blades any play in the bearings of the pump can be felt. Although repair kits are available to strip down and rebuild the pump, it is more effective to replace the complete unit as special tools and a hydraulic press will be required to dismantle it.

5.18. If the water pump on the 4-cylinder 23c and the petrol/TVO 85 mm engines needs to be removed, the rear housing attached to the engine block can be left in situ. If it is removed, then a new gasket needs to be fitted and the housing attached to the block first.

5.19. When fitting the new water pump ensure that the grease nipple for the pump bearing is facing up. Also make sure that you use a new gasket.

5.14. Radiator off

5.15. Remove TVO engine radiator

5.16. Remove fan blades

5.17. Water pump and housing

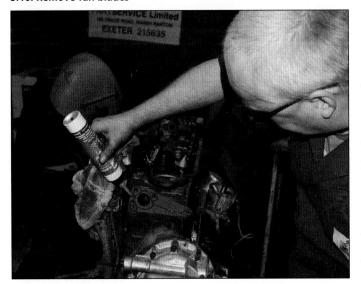

5.18. Fit new gasket

5.19. Fit new water pump for petrol /TVO engine

5.20. Corrosion on timing case

5.21 Layout of pump for 3-cylinder engine

5.22. Pulley alignment

5.20. The 3-cylinder (3.152) engine uses the aluminium timing case housing as the mounting for the water pump. If the wear plate behind the pump fails, then corrosion will occur to the housing.

5.21. An internal seal failure resulted in a water leak requiring the fitting of a new water pump – the old brass wear plate and a new gasket is being used. The four bolts securing the pump should be refitted with new copper washers and the longest bolt in the top right-hand position. Fit the short bypass hose with the pump and, as a precaution, replace all the hoses and clips to reduce the risk of breakdowns.

5.22. To ensure long fan belt life and to provide correct alignment of the belt, the pulleys should be visually checked for alignment with each other when viewed from the side of the engine.

The dynamo mounting bracket can be adjusted to ensure it is running true.

Possible Faults with the Engine Cooling System

Remember that a worn engine, incorrect ignition timing, poor maintenance and excessive overload will cause the system to be unable to work efficiently even though the cooling system may not be faulty.

SYMPTOM	POSSIBLE FAULT	REMEDY
Coolant boils and engine runs too hot	Low coolant level in radiator.	Top up and check for leaks.
	Radiator cap leaking coolant; no pressure in system.	Check condition of seals and spring and replace.
	Hoses – leaking due to damaged/perished or loose hose clip.	Inspect and replace or tighten.
	Fan blades – incorrectly fitted 'blowing not sucking' or damaged.	Replace or refit.
	Fan belt – slack or slipping.	Check belt condition and tension or replace.
	Head gasket – faulty with loss of coolant not evident due to leaks.	Remove the cylinder head and inspect/replace.
	Engine block – coolant passage internally.	Flush out system.
	Radiator – fins/core blocked.	Clean external fins and/or flush out internal core or replace unit.
	Thermostat – stuck closed.	Check operation in hot water and replace if found faulty.
Engine runs too cold	Thermostat – stuck open.	Fit new.
	Very cold operating conditions or light loads.	Fit blanking screen to radiator.
	Temperature sender reading too low or high.	Replace faulty sender and/or gauge.

Chapter 6 | Fuel Systems

This section covers both petrol/TVO and diesel 3- and 4-cylinder fuel systems as fitted to Massey Ferguson 35 tractors. It will enable the reader to understand the operation of the system parts and how to diagnose faults as well as service and repair the components. Care must be taken when working on the fuel system because of the high diesel fuel pressures and the reaction to the skin; read the safety section on page 6.

Carburettors

The carburettors used on the petrol and petrol/TVO engines are similar in appearance and the exceptions to this can be seen in the specification chart.

Air is drawn in through the oil bath air cleaner and is filtered past to the carburettor via the connection pipe. As the engine draws in air through the carburettor, the fuel enters the carburettor at the banjo union and the float chamber through the needle assembly. As the fuel rises in the chamber, the floats will be lifted until – at the predetermined fuel level – they will push the needle onto its seating and thus prevent the entry of more fuel.

Tools required for checks:

Range of imperial and/or metric spanners and socket sets

Air compressor and long reach jet

Chemical cleaner (brake cleaner)

Protective gloves or barrier hand cream

From the float chamber the fuel passes around the adjusting needle through the main jet and rises to the predetermined level in the main discharge tube, the slow running jet passage and the main air bleed passage. It is then drawn into the engine depending upon the throttle position, which controls the flow of air via the butterfly.

For ease of cold starting, a rich mixture is provided by pulling on the choke knob, this restricts the air entering the engine but allows excess fuel to be drawn into the engine to permit starting. Once warm it can be pushed in.

28G CARBURETTOR

Adjustments Petrol Engine Tractor

Main Jet	1¾ turns open ± ¼ turn
Slow Running Jet	1¾ turns open approx.

Petrol Engine Tractors will be found to be fitted with one of the following carburettors:

C-1542
Identification: Stamped C-1542. Dab of yellow paint on F.C. cover.
Data:
Choke Tube Dia.	19 mm
Main Jet	245 cc
Air Jet	.70 mm
S.R.Jet	70
Needle Seating	2.0 mm
Fuel Level	17 mm at 18" head

(measured from top face of carburettor bowl)

C-1575
Identification: Stamped C-1575. Dab of blue paint on F.C. cover, dab of green on bowl.
Data:
Choke Tube Dia.	19 mm
Main Jet	245 cc
Air Jet	.70 mm
S.R.Jet	55
Needle Seating	2.0 mm
Fuel Level	17 mm at 18" head

(measured from top face of carburettor bowl)

The carburettors fitted to the Vaporising Oil and Lamp Oil Engine Tractors are similar to those fitted on the Petrol Engine version. One of the following will be found to be fitted:

C-1575
Identification: Stamped C-1575. Dab of blue paint on F.C. cover, dab of green on bowl.
Data:
Choke Tube Dia.	19 mm
Main Jet	245 cc
Air Jet	.70 mm
S.R.Jet	55
Needle Seating	2.0 mm
Fuel Level	17 mm at 18" head

(measured from top face of carburettor bowl)

C-1578
Identification: Stamped C-1578. Dab of brown paint on F.C. cover, and on bowl.
Data:
Choke Tube Dia.	19 mm
Main Jet	245 cc
Air Jet	.70 mm
S.R.Jet	80
Needle Seating	2.0 mm
Fuel Level	17 mm at 18" head

(measured from top face of carburettor bowl)

28G CARBURETTOR

V.O. Tractor
Main Jet	2 turns open ± ¼ turn
Slow Running Jet	1¾ turns open approx.

L.O. Tractor
Main Jet	2 turns open ± ¼ turn
Slow Running Jet	1¾ turns open approx.

Carburettor Engine Fuel System Fault Table

FAULT	POSSIBLE CAUSE	ATTENTION REQUIRED
Will not start	Fuel supply restricted.	Ensure that fuel is turned on and that float needle valve is not sticking. Examine filter screens, strainers and filler cap vent for blockage. Examine sediment bowl for air-lock.
	Choke plate not closing fully.	Inspect and adjust as instructed.
	Incorrect adjustment of inter-connecting linkage between throttle and choke.	Inspect and adjust as instructed.
	Too rich a mixture due either to use of choke when engine is hot, or 'pumping' throttle hand lever when operating starter.	Push choke control fully home. Open throttle hand lever to its limits and operate starter. After first few revolutions of the engine, excess fuel will be cleared. Reset controls and engine should start.
Difficult starting – poor idling	Incorrect setting of either or both of the idler adjust screws.	Re-adjust as instructed.
	Dirt below idler jet.	Remove jet and clean by blowing out.
	Air leak due to loose manifold, carburettor unions, throttle spindle bushes or hose connections to air cleaner.	Tighten nuts, renew seals, gaskets or hoses as necessary.
	Sticking float needle.	See 'Fuel supply restricted' (above).
Poor response from engine on opening throttle	Non-standard main jet.	Fit correct main jet.
	Incorrect main jet adjustment.	Adjust according to instructions.
	Choke plate not opening fully when dash control is released.	Inspect and adjust linkage.
	Jets not screwed down tightly.	Check jets for tightness.
	Fuel level in float chamber too low.	Re-adjust float setting as required.
	Air cleaner oil bath over filled or cleaner element dirty.	Wash out air cleaner and refill oil bath to correct level with clean oil.
Leakage and flooding	Grit on float needle seating.	Caused by damaged filter screens in carburettor or fuel sediment bowl. Inspect and clean or renew screens where necessary. Remove needle and clean seating by blowing out. When re-assembling ensure that all washers are perfect and tightened adequately.
	Fuel level in float chamber too high.	Re-adjust setting as required.
	Leaking float.	Replace.

Faults occurring due to poor starting, lack of power, misfire, or excessive fuel use are best solved by stripping down, inspecting and cleaning the carburettor.

Once overhauled, the carburettor adjustment screws are set to the correct specifications. The engine is then run up to operating temperature so that the final adjustments can be made. Set the idle speed between 400 and 450 rpm. The idle mixture screw should be screwed out (to weaken the mixture) until the engine runs unevenly at which point it can be screwed back in one turn until smooth running occurs. The main jet adjustment can now be carried out by moving the screw a quarter of a turn either way from the base settings, which are dependent upon the engine and the fuel used, until smooth running under load with good power is achieved.

Overhauling the carburettor

The following pictures explain the procedure for overhauling the carburettor.

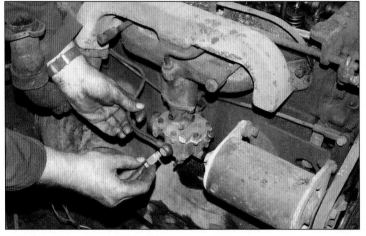

6.01. To remove the carburettor, first turn off the fuel and disconnect the fuel line banjo bolt. Then disconnect the governor linkage and the air cleaner pipe.

6.01. Disconnect the carburettor

6.02. Disconnect linkage

6.02. Remove the throttle and choke linkage. It will be easier to do this after the carburettor has been unbolted from the inlet manifold.

6.03. Layout of 28G carburettor components.

6.04. Throttle and choke linkage connections: when the choke is operated, the link rod slightly raises the idle speed of the engine for smooth cold running.

6.05. To remove corrosion and accumulated dirt, use a mild caustic solution or a carburettor cleaner.

6.06. Remove the idle mixture jet and note the number of turns. Keep the spring with the jet. Check the tapered end for damage and built-up dirt.

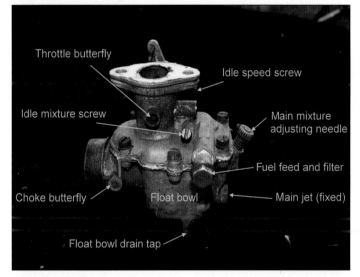

Throttle butterfly

Idle speed screw

Idle mixture screw

Main mixture adjusting needle

Fuel feed and filter

Choke butterfly   Float bowl   Main jet (fixed)

Float bowl drain tap

6.03. Front view

Throttle rod connection

Link rod

Choke lever connection

6.04. Rear view

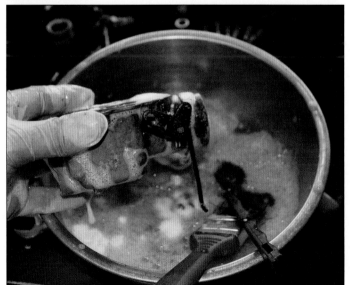

6.05. Chemical clean

6.06. Idle mixture jet

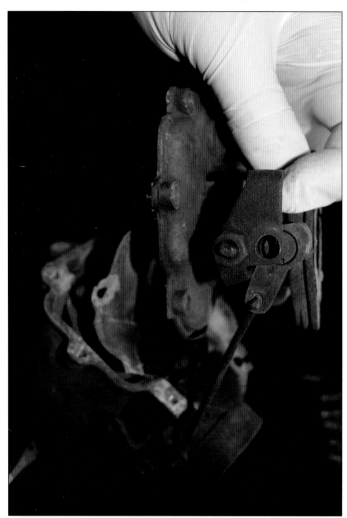

6.07. Remove top cover

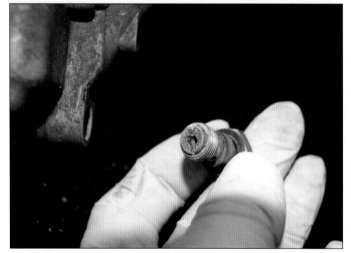

6.10. Fixed main jet

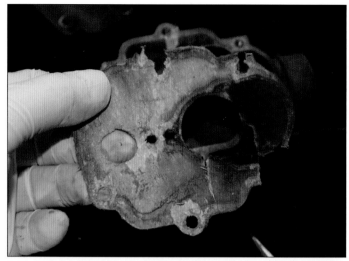

6.08. Gasket

6.09. Float

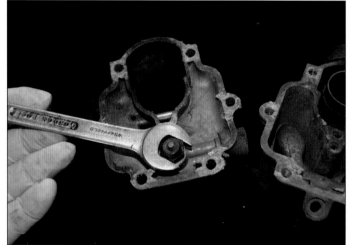

6.11. Float needle

6.07. Remove the screws securing the carburettor top cover and unclip the choke linkage.

6.08. Upon removing the cover, it is common to find a damaged gasket. Therefore, it is advisable to order and fit a new gasket for the rebuild.

6.09. Carefully lift out the dual float and pivot pin and submerse in clean fuel. Also check that the part floats: if it allows fuel to leak inside, it will not work and a replacement will need to be fitted.

6.10. The fixed main jet fits in the bottom of the float chamber and any dirt in the float chamber is very likely to block this jet.

6.12. Main discharge tube

6.13. Main jet

6.14. Slow running and air bleed jets

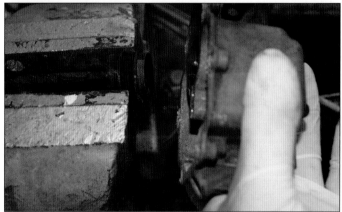

6.15. Remove venturi

6.16. Remove spindle old bushes

6.17. New bushes to throttle

Therefore, it is important to clean with compressed air and carburettor cleaner.

6.11. By blowing through the inlet banjo fitting, you can check that the float needle is performing as it should. However, the carburettor overhaul kit includes this part so it is easy to replace.

6.12. The main discharge tube is where the fuel emerges into the air flow to the engine. It has very small holes that need to be cleaned carefully.

6.13. Unscrew the main mixture jet and check for blockages in the hole. Also check for wear on the end of the taper.

6.14. These two small jets control the main air bleed to the main jet (right hand) and the slow running jet (left hand).

6.15. To enable a full clean of the carburettor internals, the venturi can be pulled out of the main body.

6.16. Play in the throttle spindle will cause fluctuating air flow through the carburettor; the overhaul kit includes new plastic bushes to replace the worn ones as well as a new spindle and butterfly. First remove the butterfly screws and throttle linkage, then withdraw the spindle.

6.17. Fit the new plastic bushes into the spindle hole by gently tapping them in until they are flush.

6.18. Disconnect linkage

6.19. New throttle spindle and bushes

6.20. Float level

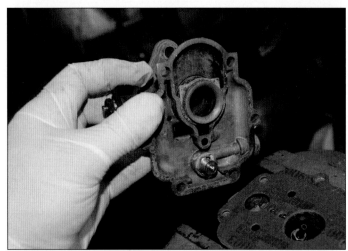

6.21. New gasket

6.18. Slide in the new spindle and check for smooth movement, then refit the throttle linkage. Insert the butterfly into the slot in the spindle.

6.19. Turn the spindle until the butterfly sits squarely in the carburettor housing and then tighten the screws. Check for smooth movement.

6.20. When reassembling the carburettor, the float level needs to be checked. A mark 17 mm from the top of the chamber is made and when the float chamber is full of liquid (preferably non-flammable for this test) the top of the float should be parallel to this line. Bend the pivot to adjust the level.

6.21. Always replace the gasket upon overhaul as air and fuel leaks will cause problems with the running of the engine.

6.22. With the carburettor cleaned, reset and rebuilt a new gasket is fitted between the manifold and the carburettor. The linkages are reconnected and the main mixture screw and the slow running, or idle mixture screw, are set to the specifications of the engine being used.

6.22. Ready to fit

Fuel Lift Pump Overhaul

The mechanical lift pumps fitted to the Massey Ferguson diesel tractors are mounted on the side of the engine and driven by the camshaft lobe. On the 3-cylinder engine, the pump incorporates a glass bowl so dirt and water contamination can be easily seen and eradicated.

The pumps both operate in the same manner: as the engine rotates, the camshaft lobe forces the arm of the pump to move down pulling the diaphragm (against a return spring), which causes a vacuum to be produced. This opens the inlet valve and the fuel, under atmospheric pressure, flows into the space above the diaphragm. As the camshaft rotates, the pump arm is free and the return spring forces the diaphragm upwards closing the inlet valve and opening the outlet valve. This forces the fuel out to the fuel system under pressure of up to 0.7 bar (10 psi). The cycle is then repeated.

The pump produces a constant pressure, but if the diesel fuel system does not require it, i.e. when idling, then the back pressure can hold the diaphragm down. This allows the pump to effectively idle – due to the internal connecting link between the arm and the diaphragm – even though the arm is still being moved by the camshaft. An external manual pumping lever is supplied to enable fuel to be forced through when bleeding the diesel fuel system.

To inspect the fuel lift pump, remove the two fuel pipes. Note their relevant positions and then unbolt them from the engine

block. Plug the two open connections and wash off the outside of the pump and clean with an air line.

Note: due to the low cost of the pump, internal spares are difficult to obtain and usually a complete new pump can be purchased and fitted. Disassembling the fuel pump is useful when it is likely that the internal faults are due to the accumulation of dirt. In these cases, the build-up can be cleared and the pump will function as normal.

To carry out a simple check of the pump's operation: remove it from the engine, place your finger over the outlet and operate the hand lever. You should feel pressure pushing against you. Then place your finger over the inlet and, similarly, you should feel suction when the hand lever is operated.

The procedure for stripping down the fuel lift pump for closer inspection is the same for both 3- and 4-cylinder diesel engines. Follow the pictorial process.

6.23. Mark the two housings

6.23. To allow the top halves of the housings to be refitted in the correct orientation always score the two halves of the pump. Note: when purchasing a new lift pump it may be necessary to remove the top housing and rotate it into the correct position so that the pipe fittings match the old pump.

6.24. Remove diaphragm

6.24. Remove the diaphragm by pushing down and twisting until it unclips from the operating rod. Then lift out the return spring.

6.25. Inspect diaphragm

6.26. In and out valves

6.27. Threads in housing

6.28. Remove glass bowl

6.25. Inspect the diaphragm for splits or perishing on its surface. If the diaphragm fails, the engine may still operate but the oil level in the engine may increase. Otherwise, the fuel could be seen leaking below the pump body.

6.26. The inlet and outlet valves are simple fibre washers with a lift spring holding them in the closed position. The fuel pressure provides the correct sealing. If dirt particles become trapped in the valve, they may hold the valve open, which means that the pump will not operate effectively. Clean the inlet and outlet valves with a low pressure air jet.

6.27. The soft aluminium housing sometimes makes it difficult to align the fuel pipes into the threads when refitting the pump. It is common to find cross-threading, which will allow air into the system or fuel to leak out of the pump. If either of these is found, a replacement pump should be fitted.

6.28. The 3-cylinder diesel engine uses a glass bowl extension to the fuel pump housing – although the pump internals are the same as the previous pictures. Unscrew the retaining clip and remove the bowl. Then wash out

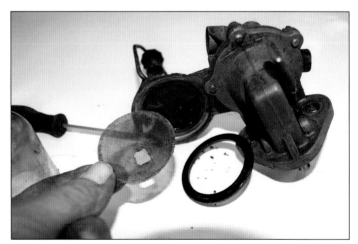

6.29. Gauze filter

any sludge or water and check the condition of the rubber sealing washer.

6.29. To maintain the gauze filter, remove it from the top of the glass bowl, wash and gently clean with a low pressure air jet.

3-cylinder Diesel Fuel System

The diesel engine fuel system components are manufactured to tolerances of as little as 0.0025 mm. They supply, transfer, clean and deliver fuel to the engine cylinders to enable combustion, thereby producing power. The fuel injection pump produces pressures in the range of 100 to 185 bar (1,500 to 2,720 psi). These high pressures are necessary to ensure the diesel injectors give optimum atomisation to the fuel to enable a complete fuel burn; this is essential for achieving good power and fuel usage.

The diesel engine uses the compression of air to produce enough heat to ignite the fuel; therefore, it is important that the fuel injector sprays a very fine mist into the hot air to enable the engine to start and run correctly.

When did you last have your injectors checked? Manufacturers recommend that injectors are checked and/ or serviced approximately every one thousand hours of operation. You are unlikely to notice the loss of power, but you may notice that the engine is running unevenly or noisily; that it has difficulty starting; or that it is overheating, smoking, or using more fuel than it used to.

Diesel injectors can suffer from varnish deposits, clogging, wear and leakage. Today's low sulphur diesel fuels are more likely to leave varnish and gum deposits on injectors. They also provide less lubrication. Dirty injectors will lean out the air/fuel mixture, causing a loss of power, rough idle and sometimes white smoke in the exhaust. Leaky injectors will enrich the air/fuel mixture, causing black smoke, and speed up the engine wear due to fuel washing lubrication oil away from cylinder walls. (See page 105 on servicing fuel injectors.)

Filtration

Diesel fuel system contamination is a common problem. The most common contaminants found in the diesel fuel are:

Organic elements – oxidation or degradation of the fuel with age.

Micro-organisms – growth can occur when a mixture of water and diesel fuel sits idle for any extended period of time (common in vintage tractor diesel tanks). These micro-organisms live in the water, feed off the diesel fuel, and can thrive in any fuel/water. This is sometimes called black sludge.

Water – in fuel can be found in two forms:

Free water is water that is not mixed in the fuel and will settle out over a short period of time at the bottom of the fuel tank or filter housing/glass bowl.

Emulsified water is mixed in the fuel and much harder to remove. This bonding with the fuel occurs as the fuel/water mixture passes through a fuel lift pump.

Inorganic elements – component wear materials, rust, scale and dirt. This contamination can cause the most damage to the fuel system components due to its hard and abrasive nature.

Storage

Obviously, contamination can be avoided by regularly using fresh fuel in the tractor and by ensuring that the diesel has a clean storage system. Unfortunately vintage tractors tend to have prolonged periods of inactivity and therefore it is important to do one of two things: either run the diesel fuel down in the tractor before it is stored over winter or refill the tank with fresh, new fuel for the period of use. Additives can help prolong the life of diesel fuel.

Fuel filters and water separators

The purpose of any diesel fuel filter is to remove any common contaminants, such as the ones previously listed. The use of a suitable filtration system on diesel engines is a must to avoid damage to closely fitted injection pump and injector components. On tractor diesel engines a primary and secondary filter is used. The primary filter is capable of removing dirt particles down to about 0.05 to 0.03 mm (50 to 30 microns) and the secondary filter between 0.01 to 0.12 mm (10 to 12 microns). Secondary filters, fitted to tractors from around the 1980s, will filter down to between 3 and 5 microns. The primary is usually located between the tank and the supply pump and the secondary filter between the supply pump and the injection pump.

Water separators or agglomerators

Too much water in a fuel filter will render it incapable of protecting the system. So to ensure this does not happen, some diesel engine fuel systems are equipped with fuel filter/water separators for the purpose of trapping and holding water that may be mixed in with the fuel. The first stage of the fuel filter/water separator uses a pleated paper element to change the small water particles, which have been squashed by the lift pump, into large enough droplets (agglomerates) that they will succumb to gravity and fall into a water sump at the bottom of the filter.

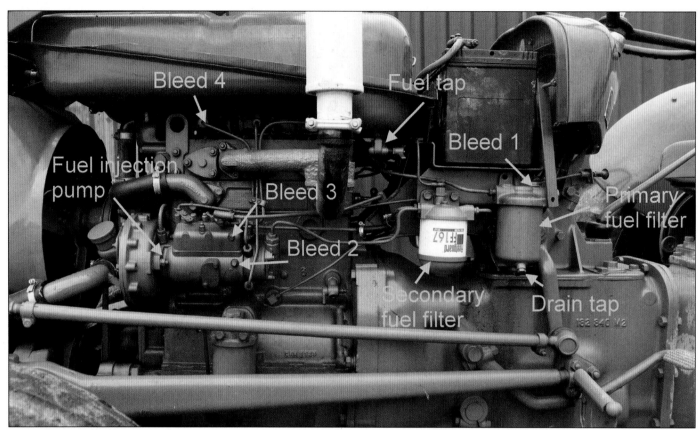

6.30. 3-cylinder diesel left-hand view

6.31. 3-cylinder diesel right-hand view

6.32. Remove filter

6.33. Replacing fuel filter

6.34. Replacing filter seals

The second stage of the agglomerator is made of silicone-treated nylon that acts as a safety mechanism by preventing small particles of water – those that avoided the first stage – passing into the injection pump. This water will fall to the bottom of the filter (glass) bowl and can be drained out as required.

6.30. After changing any components or filters the fuel system will need to be bled. This means that all the air in the fuel system needs to be removed otherwise the engine will not start.

First ensure you have at least half a tank of fuel and the fuel tap turned on. Then open the bleed screw on top of the filter housing (1) and pump fuel via the fuel lift pump priming lever (mounted on the right-hand side of the engine) until only fuel runs out of the bleed screw. Tighten the screw.

Slacken the small bleed screw (2) on front of the fuel injection pump. Then operate the lift pump again until only fuel runs out. Tighten and repeat on top screw (3).

Slacken the injector pipe union (4) a quarter of a turn and start the engine with the fuel cut-off lever in run position and the throttle lever fully open. Tighten the union, but beware of fuel spurting from the injection union. Then run the engine for a few minutes checking the system for leaks and correct running.

6.31. The small reservoir (at the rear of the fuel tank) for the thermostart cold starting device is topped up with fuel from the fuel filter housing. When the ignition key is turned to the left, spring-loaded position power is supplied to the thermostart and

6.35. Refitting fuel filters

this causes it to heat. It then burns the diesel fuel and a hot flame enters the engine to aid cold temperature starting.

6.32. To service and prolong the life of the fuel system it is necessary to replace the cartridge element fuel filter located on the left-hand side of the tractor. This filter prevents dirt and water from damaging the fuel injection parts.

6.33. In this picture, the dirt and rust has accumulated at the base of the bowl. The origin of the sediment and rust needs to be found – it could possibly be a rusty internal diesel fuel tank – and cured to prevent damaged to the injectors and pump.

6.34. Ensure you replace the seals, which come supplied with the filter, to prevent fuel leaks and poor running due to air leaks. Refit the new filter, remembering to clean out the lower housing that collects sediment and dirt from the system. A drain tap is fitted to the base to allow the removal of water from the system without the need for bleeding.

6.35. There should be four seals in the filter box to be replaced: two small 'o' rings for the top of the filter housing and two for the filter. The slightly

6.36. Refit filter

smaller of the two fits in the lower bowl and the larger one fits up inside the filter housing.

6.36. When refitting the fuel filter ensure the seals align correctly and that the centre screw is not over tightened.

6.37. Some tractors use a paper element inside a steel housing. Ensure that you replace the old seal with the new one

6.37. Fitting fuel filters

6.38. Filter in rotary injection pump

supplied with the filter. This will help to prevent fuel leaks and poor running caused by air leaks. Refit the new filter, remembering to put the various sealing washers and springs in the correct position and clean out the housing that will collect sediment and dirt in the system.

6.38. A last resort in the fight against dirt and contaminants is the filter fitted in the rear of the rotary injection pump.

6.39. Timing of rotary injection pump

6.40. Fitting injection pump

Unfortunately if it is found to be blocked then damage to the pump has probably started to occur. To check it, remove the feed fuel pipe and unscrew the large union. Then pop the filter out using your little finger and clean if necessary.

6.39. To check the timing of the diesel fuel injection pump, first remove the rubber plug from the left-hand side of the bell housing. Next turn the engine over until the number one cylinder is on the compression stroke, i.e. both valves are closed. The 18 degrees mark, 'SPILL

18', should be visible. Remove the side inspection cover of the pump and the letter 'E' should be aligned with the edge (or scribe line) on the circlip.

6.40. If the timing marks on the gears are correct, then the pump can be fitted and removed without disturbing the timing as there is a slot machined into the drive of the injection pump which fits into the dowel on the timing gear. The three set screws can now be fitted to the timing case and the scribed lines on the case and pump aligned to give the correct timing position.

6.41. Fuel tank tap fit

6.41. There is a filter fitted to the inlet of the fuel tap to prevent dirt entering the system. It is best checked when the fuel tank level is fairly low.

4-cylinder Diesel Fuel System

The Massey Ferguson 4-cylinder 23c engine fuel system has a 34 litre (7.5 gallon) fuel tank that supplies fuel to the on/off tap at the rear of the tank. There is one filter fitted inside the tank. Fuel passes to the engine drive mechanical lift pump, which also has a gauze internal filter, and onto the single fuel filter. After being thoroughly cleaned, the diesel enters the fuel injection pump at the rear pipe and then, under high pressure, it is distributed to the relevant injector. Excess fuel at the injectors is used to cool and lubricate; then it is returned to the pipe fitted in the lower part of the fuel tank.

Fuel passing through the fuel injection pump lubricates and cools and then returns via the front pipe to the fuel filter housing. A small reservoir at the rear of the fuel tank supplies the cold start thermostart with a constant feed of fuel to allow ease of starting in temperatures lower than 4 °Celsius.

Stripping down and cleaning the injectors and fitting them with new nozzle tips is considered a sufficient overhaul. They

🔧 Tools required for checks:

Range of imperial spanners and ⅜ and ½ sockets

7 mm (⁵⁄₁₆ in) socket screw

Gasket sealer

must also be adjusted for opening pressure and should have their spray pattern checked using an injector 'pop' tester. (See page 105 for the procedure.) This will assist with the smooth running of engines generally, and help to overcome the poor starting characteristic of this engine in particular.

6.42. After changing any components or filters the fuel system will need to be bled. It is important to remove all the air in the fuel system because otherwise the engine will not start.

First ensure you have at least half a tank of fuel and the fuel tap turned on. Open the bleed screw on top of the filter housing (1) and pump the fuel via the fuel lift pump priming lever (mounted on the left-hand side of engine) until all that runs out of the bleed screw is fuel. Then tighten the screw.

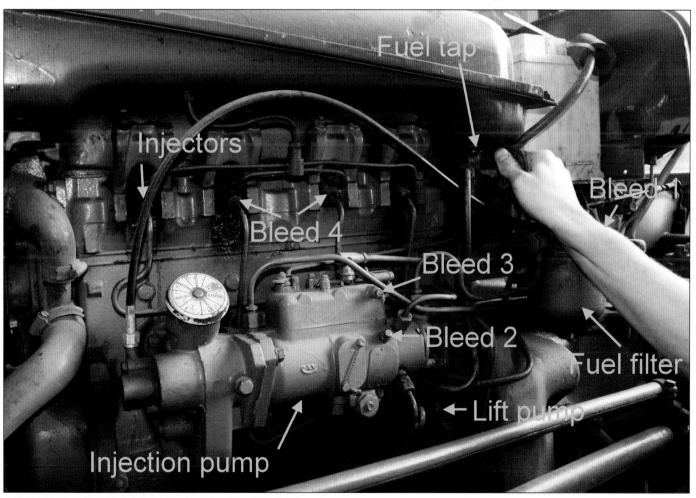

6.42. 4-cylinder diesel left-hand view has the three bleed points shown

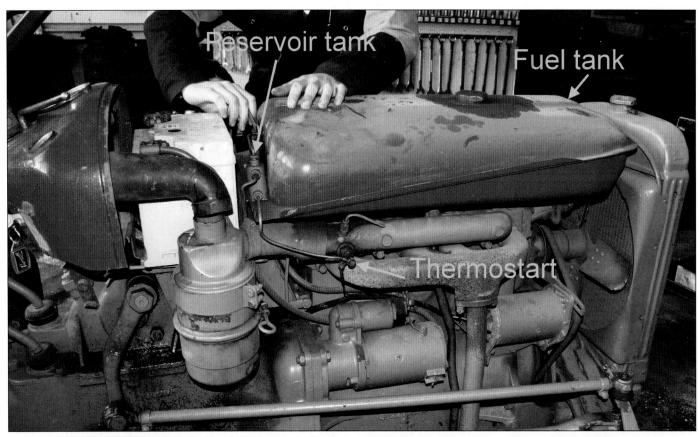

6.43. 4-cylinder diesel right-hand view

6.44. Injector removal

Slacken the small bleed screw (2) on the front of the fuel injection pump and operate the lift pump again until only fuel runs out. Tighten and repeat on top screw (3).

Slacken the injector pipes union (4) a quarter of a turn and start the engine with the fuel cut-off lever in run position and the throttle lever fully open. Tighten the union and run the engine, checking the system for leaks and correct running. Beware of fuel spurting from the injection union when tightening.

6.43. The small reservoir for the thermostart cold starting device is topped up with fuel from the fuel filter housing.

6.45. Pump drive master spline

When the ignition key is turned to the left against spring pressure, battery voltage is supplied to the thermostart. It heats up the internal element then burns the diesel fuel and a hot flame enters the engine, heating the air within the cylinder to aid cold temperature starting.

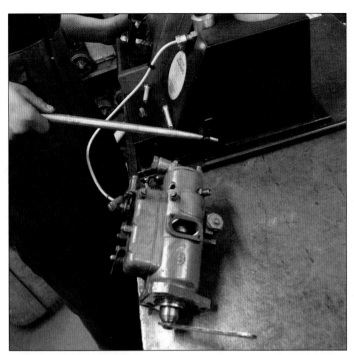

6.46. Check timing marks

6.44. Mark each injector starting with number one at the water pump end of the engine. This is the standard numbering procedure for all rebuilds. Then slacken off the retaining nuts evenly, lift off the bridging pieces and gently prise the injectors out of the head. Make a note that the copper sealing washer will need to be removed from the hole before replacing the injectors.

6.45. If the engine has been rebuilt and a new timing chain fitted to ensure correct fuel pump timing then, with the timing cover removed and the timing marks aligned, turn the engine anticlockwise until the number one piston is halfway down the bore. Refit the flywheel with new lock tabs and ensure the locating dowel in the crankshaft fits the flywheel. On the left-hand side of the engine is a small hole in the rear case. Slide a 6.3 mm (¼ in) dowel into the casing, then rotate the engine clockwise and the dowel should slide into a corresponding hole in the flywheel, locking the engine at 16 degrees before TDC. Fit the injection pump drive housing onto the block (with a new gasket) and by turning the gear, which is driven from the camshaft, position the master spline drive to approximately 45 degrees to the vertical as shown.

6.46. Before the injection pump can be fitted to the pump housing, the side inspection cover is removed to view the timing letter on the pump rotor. The letter 'G' should align with the line scribed on the internal circlip. If not it will be necessary to fit the pump to a 'pop' tester. Once that has been done we can pressure the outlet pipe to the number one injector, lock the pump into the correct position and make a timing mark on the circlip. This would normally have to be carried out by a fuel injection specialist if you do not have the necessary equipment.

6.47. With the flywheel locating dowel fitted and the master spline on the pump drive at 45 degrees, the fuel injection pump with a new gasket can be fitted. Align the two scribed marks on the

6.47. Fit injection pump

6.48. Timing cover fit

6.49. Connecting fuel lines

housing and the pump body. You should find the internal letter (G) will also be in the correct position with the internal circlip. Any adjustment can be made by rotating the pump slightly on the mounting flange.

6.48. Rotate the engine two revolutions and check that all the timing marks realign. Any slight adjustment can be made by rotating the injection pump body. Refit the inspection cover on the pump with a new gasket. Then fit the timing cover with a new gasket and locate the cover on the dowels. Fit all the bolts loosely and then slide on the front pulley. Then tighten the bolts evenly. This procedure will align the new front seal with the front pulley to allow it to seal correctly.

6.49. The final task before starting the engine is to attach all the ancillaries, such as fuel lines, fuel lift pump, manifolds, water

6.50. Fuel tank tap fit

6.51. Fuel filter layout

pump, thermostart housing and starter motor. Then the diesel tank can be fitted onto the top of the engine.

The injector can now be fitted with new copper sealing washers and tightened evenly to 25–28 Nm (18–22 lb-ft).

6.50. A gauze tube filter is fitted to the top of the fuel tank tap; this prevents dirt, which has accumulated in the tank, from progressing on to the fuel system where it could potentially damage or block the components. If the fuel flow is found to be low or the engine is difficult to bleed after servicing, then the filter should be removed and cleaned or replaced.

6.51. The 4-cylinder diesel engine utilises a single large fuel filter and the various seals should be replaced upon servicing as shown in the picture.

Air Cleaner Operation and Service

Checking and servicing the air filter system are two of the most important jobs that you can do to maintain your tractor. A petrol/TVO engine will need approximately 9,000 gallons of air to 1 gallon of fuel, while diesel engines require significantly more air. A clean air filter ensures that the tractor is running at its most efficient in terms of power produced: not only will it efficiently use fuel but it will also prevent damage, which could be caused by lack of air in the engine. A blocked air filter resulting in insufficient air intake will lead to fuel dilution of the engine oil. This in turn will cause accelerated engine wear of the bores, piston rings and bearings.

🔧 Tools required for checks:

Range of imperial and/or metric spanners and socket sets

Air compressor and jet

Chemical cleaner (brake cleaner)

Protective gloves or barrier hand cream

The oil bath wire mesh type air filter fitted to the Massey Ferguson tractor is efficient at removing 88% of the dirt from the incoming air. Its main advantage is that no special tools or parts are required to service it. A mushroom-domed pre-cleaner is fitted to some models; as its name suggests, this pre-cleaner removes large particles of dust and dirt to prevent blockages to the main air cleaner if the tractor is working in very dusty conditions. The pre-cleaner is positioned above the tractor bonnet in an area where less dust and dirt accumulates.

The service intervals for the air cleaner will vary depending upon the operating conditions, i.e. the amount of dust, chaff and dirt that the tractor encounters. The filter may require attention every five hours in very dusty conditions!

6.52. The oil bath air cleaner is simple in construction. The dirty air is drawn down the centre pipe (via a pre-cleaner if fitted) as the engine is started. As it reaches the bottom of the housing it is forced to do a U-turn, which throws heavier particles of dirt into the oil bath. As the air continues upwards some of the oil is drawn up with it. This oil is then trapped in the wire mesh, which filters out any further particles. The cleaned air goes through to the engine via a rubber connection pipe, while the dirty oil trapped in the wire falls back into the oil bath taking the dirt with it.

6.53. This engine oil bath filter has not been serviced regularly and grass and straw have built

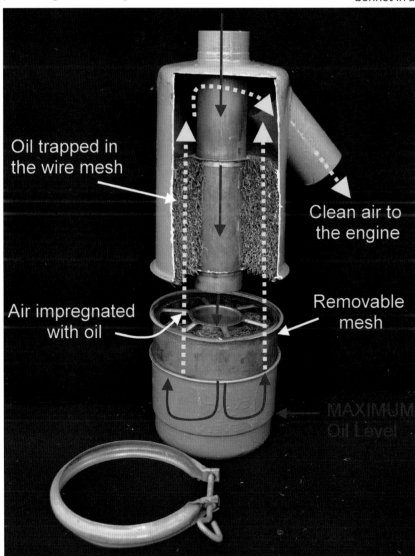

Oil trapped in the wire mesh

Clean air to the engine

Air impregnated with oil

Removable mesh

MAXIMUM Oil Level

6.52. Oil bath air cleaner

6.53. Dirty oil bath filter

6.54. Sludge in bowl

6.55. Refilling with clean oil

6.56. Collapsed air pipe

up in the wire mesh. It will be necessary to remove the filter, wash it out with paraffin or diesel and then spray it with a high pressure hose. Allow the filter to dry and then reassemble.

6.54. After removing the clamp the lower bowl can be removed and the oil inspected. This is typical of a tractor working in normal conditions over approximately 10 to 20 hours.

6.55. Fill with 0.57 litres (1 pint) of clean engine oil to maximum mark only. If the bowl is overfilled the engine could draw the oil into the combustion causing it to over-rev which could result in serious damage. The intervals for cleaning depend upon the conditions in which the tractor is working; in very dusty conditions the part may need cleaning several times a day. Warning signs include loss of power and black exhaust smoke.

6.56. Check the rubber pipe and clips connecting the oil bath air filter to the engine. This one has perished, split and collapsed causing a restriction to the engine and therefore reducing the engine power.

Diesel Fuel Injectors

Manufacturers recommend that injectors are checked/serviced approximately every 500 hours of operation. Due to the long period in between checks you will not notice a loss of power, rather the engine may appear to run unevenly or more noisily or may have difficulty starting. A few other symptoms that might be noticeable are overheating, smoking or using more fuel than before.

Diesel engines use compression of air to produce enough heat to ignite the fuel so it is very important that the fuel injector sprays a very fine mist into the hot air to enable the engine to start and run correctly.

Diesel injectors are susceptible to varnish deposits, clogging, wear and leakage. Today's low sulphur diesel fuels are more likely to leave varnish and gum deposits on injectors and also provide less lubrication.

Dirty injectors will lean out the air/fuel mixture, causing a loss of power, rough idle and sometimes white smoke in the exhaust. Leaky injectors will enrich the air/fuel mixture, causing black smoke, and speed up engine wear due to fuel washing lubrication oil away from cylinder walls.

The diesel injectors used in the Massey Ferguson 4- and 3-cylinder engines operate at opening pressures of 130 and 120 bar (1,784 to 1,740 psi). Over time, their opening pressure can drop. It is considered acceptable for the opening pressure to drop by up to 10 bar (150 psi) but if the pressure drops by more, then the injectors should be replaced or reset back to their original operating specs. You will need an injector pop tester to check the opening pressure of the injectors if you suspect this kind of problem. Sykes Pickavant supplies the latest version with an extraction system to remove mist from the calibration fluid. Alternatively, you may be lucky to find a second-hand version in an auction or on eBay (you seem to be able to bid for just about anything on this!).

Care must be taken when using these machines: eye, mouth and hand safety equipment must be worn at all times. There should never be naked flames (i.e. smoking) present in the same area. Injectors can produce very high pressures – enough to inject fuel into your skin causing blood poisoning and death!

In order to service the injectors they have to be removed from the engine. All high and low pressure pipes attached to them also need to be removed. You should take care to make a note of their locations.

Gently and evenly pry off the injector from its hole in the cylinder head. If it refuses to move, refit the locating bolts/nuts and crank over the engine – hopefully the compression will 'pop' the injector. Use masking tape to identify each injector if trying to determine a fault with the engine (cylinder).

The type of injector will depend upon the engine design. For example, the indirect injection engine used in the 4-cylinder (23c engine) tractor utilises a single-hole (pintuax) injector. If you have access to a pop tester then you can strip down and clean/inspect the injectors. Alternatively, if you do not have a pop tester most large towns will have a diesel injection specialist who will recondition your injectors for between £30 and £60 each, depending upon type.

When testing the injector, make sure you are wearing protective gear. Connect the injector to the pop tester and open the side valve. Then operate the pumping handle and inspect the spray pattern: it should be even and fine with all holes working. You should hear a buzzing noise coming from the injector at the respective opening pressures.

Hold the pressure just under the opening setting, wipe the tip of the injector clean and hold the pressure for one minute. The tip should be dry. If not the nozzle seat is leaking and will need cleaning or replacing.

The third test is nozzle leak back: hold the pressure again just under the opening pressure and allow it to drop. If the gauge drops quickly, i.e. from 130 to 90 bar in less than ten seconds, the nozzle needs attention or replacement. If any of the tests prove inconclusive then you should strip the injector for further inspection.

Before stripping the injectors ensure that they are thoroughly clean on the outside using a chemical wash, such as Jizer. To strip the injector, first remove the cap and the adjusting nut. Take out the spring and spindle and then, using a vice or holding clamp and very tight-fitting spanner, remove the nozzle retaining cap.

Separate the needle from the nozzle body and check for burning/brown marks, which are an indication that the engine has overheated at some point. Also look out for grey wear marks on the tip of the nozzle. Both faults will mean that the complete nozzle will need replacing.

Cleaning of carbon deposits on the nozzle can be achieved using a soft brass brush and brass cleaning tools from a specialist's kit. A probe can also be used to clean blocked holes in the nozzle tip, but this takes a steady hand!

If the nozzle is found to be worn then a replacement can be obtained from local fuel injection companies, but they will need to know the identification number on the nozzle body.

If the face on the injector body is scored or worn you must flatten and clean it before refitting the nozzle – the locating pins can usually be pulled out using pliers.

When rebuilding the injector it is important that it be spotlessly clean. Locate the nozzle body onto the locating pins hole upright; you will find

6.57. Modern pop tester

that it will only fit in one way. Then screw down the nozzle cap, tighten with a spanner and replace the spindle, spring and adjusting nut.

Connect the injector to a pop tester and adjust opening pressure, spray pattern, seat leakage and leak back. A good strong buzzing noise should be audible.

Refit the cap with a new copper washer and always replace the injector leak off and sealing seat copper washers with new ones.

When fitting to the engine, use a taper punch to extract the copper washer from the injector hole in the cylinder head. Then bleed the fuel system and start the engine. You should notice power and reduced smoke as well as the ease with which the engine starts.

6.57. In a Sykes Pickavant pop tester the injector is placed in a clamp and spray is collected by an extraction system. The pressure gauge will register the opening or crack-off pressure of the fuel injector.

6.58. These are the common names of the injector parts used on the 3-cylinder engines. The names of the parts will be the same for the 4-cylinder engine but the body and injector nozzle is a different type.

6.59. The 4-cylinder engine utilises a slightly different injector body and nozzle/needle, though the layout of the components is similar to the 3-cylinder injector.

6.60. The 3-cylinder engine uses a two-hole nozzle tip and when checking the operation on the pop tester the fuel should atomise cleanly from each hole. If this is not the case, then the nozzle should be cleaned or replaced.

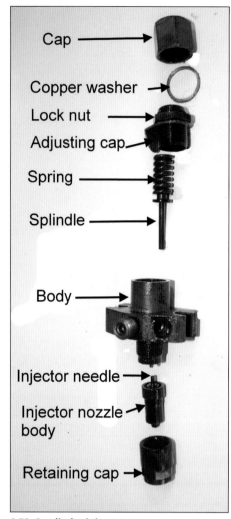

6.58. 3-cylinder injector

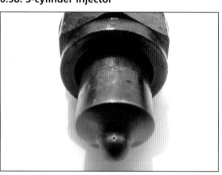

6.60. Two hole nozzle for 3-cylinder engine

6.61. The 4-cylinder engine uses a single central hole in the injector nozzle. It has an auxiliary spray hole on the (left-hand) side of the tip. This spray hole can be used with a low cranking engine speed to assist in cold starting. (You would spray fuel onto a heater element if one were fitted.)

6.62. This specialist equipment will allow you to clean the nozzle and the needle parts. You can also unblock holes in

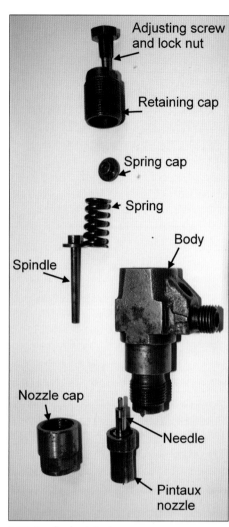

6.59. 4-cylinder injector

6.61. Single hole pintaux

tip of nozzle – if your eyes are good enough!

6.63. Home-made clamps hold the injector in the vice securely to ease the stripping process. Start at the top and work down, laying out parts as you go. Make sure to only strip down one injector at a time.

6.64. Remove the retaining cap and copper washer if fitted.

6.65. Lift out the spring and spindle.

6.62. Cleaning kit

6.63. Strip down injector

6.64. Remove lock nut

6.65. Spring and spindle

6.66. Nozzle retaining cap

6.67. Nozzle tip condition

6.66. Hold the injector body securely in the vice or holding jig and slacken the nozzle retaining cap. Note: it will be very tight. Clean all the parts so that they can be inspected. Determine whether they are suitable for reuse.

6.67. The injector body shows grey lines and brown water corrosion where the nozzle sits and the needle tip shows signs of scoring. Therefore, the nozzle and the needle need to be replaced and the body refurbished before reassembly.

6.68. Flattening face

6.69. Worn face

6.68. To remove scoring on the face of the nozzle body a flat surface, e.g. glass, and a very fine paste is used. Trace a figure of eight motion with the nozzle until the surface is flat.

6.69. The face of the injector body where the nozzle attaches forms a high-pressure seal and must be perfectly flat. By using a glass sheet and a very fine paste it can be polished flat and smooth again.

6.70. Numbers are stamped in each injector nozzle body to identify the specific type for each engine. Make sure to always quote the correct numbers when you are looking for replacement parts. Ensure that all numbers are the same for each injector in the engine.

6.70. Injector identification numbers

For 3.152 3-cylinder engine injector settings:

Atomisers

Code 3.152	Holder	Nozzle	Setting Pressure			Check and Reset Pressure		
			kgf/cm²	bar	lbf/in²	kgf/cm²	bar	lbf/in²
DD	BKB35S5258	BDL110S6133	129	125	1840	124	120	1760
DE	BKB35S5258	BDL110S6267	129	125	1840	124	120	1760
GC	BKB35SD5259	BDL110S6709	191	185	2720	176	170	2500
GW	BKB35SD5258	BDL110S6709	191	185	2720	176	170	2500

For 4-cylinder 23c engine injector settings:

Injectors

Early engines –
without heat shields.   Up to Engine No. SJ 8604SE.
   Nozzle Holders   ...   CAV type BKB 40S 697
   Nozzles   ...   ...   CAV type BDN 12SP 6169
   Working pressure 130 bar.
   Initial Setting (new injectors) 135 bar.

Engines fitted
with heat shields.   ...   Engine No. SJ B6046E to SJ 125724E.
   Nozzle Holders   ...   CAV type BKB 40S 697K
   Nozzles   ...   ...   CAV type BDN 12SP 6169 A
   or BDN 12SP 6262.
   Working pressure 130 bar.
   Initial Setting (new injectors) 135 bar.

   No. SJ 125725E and subsequent.
Nozzle Holders   ...   CAV type BKB 40S 697K
Nozzles   ...   ...   CAV type BDN 12SP 6290.
   Working pressure 130 bar.
   Initial Setting (new injectors) 135 bar.

DPA Type Distributor Fuel Injection Pump

Overhaul and repairs to the fuel injection pump can only be carried out by a fuel system specialist because of the equipment required to re-calibrate the pump after the rebuild. The only adjustment available is to check the operation of the stop lever and set the idle speed of the engine.

In the (rotary) distributor type injection pump the fuel is pumped by a single element. The fuel charges are distributed in the correct firing order and at the required timing interval to each cylinder in turn by means of a rotary distributor, integral with the pump. Therefore equal delivery of fuel to each injector is an intrinsic feature of these pumps and deliveries are not subject to maladjustment as commonly found with inline fuel injection pumps. Similarly, since the timing interval between injection strokes is determined by the accurate spacing of distribution ports and high precision operating cams that are not subject to adjustment, accurate phasing is achieved.

The pump is a compact, oil-tight unit, lubricated throughout by diesel oil and requires no separate lubrication system. Sensitive speed control is maintained by a mechanical governor operated inside the pump.

Variation of injection timing, which is required on some later engine applications, can be obtained on models of the pump that are fitted with an advance device. This advance device is fitted on the lower part of the pump and is fully automatic, requiring no attention from the operator.

Metering of fuel

Fuel entering the pump through the inlet connection on the pump end plate passes through a fine gauze filter to the inlet side of the vane-type transfer pump. The fuel pressure is then raised to an intermediate level, known as transfer pressure (0 to 100 psi), and is controlled by a piston-type regulating valve housed in the end plate. Transfer pressure does not remain constant but increases with the speed of rotation of the pump. Fuel at transfer pressure then passes through a passage in the hydraulic head to an annular groove in the rotor and then to a chamber which houses the metering valve.

The metering valve is operated by the control lever and regulates the flow of fuel through the metering port into the pumping section of the rotor. The volume of fuel passing into the pumping element is thus controlled by the transfer pressure, the position of the metering valve and the time during which an inlet port in the rotor is aligned with the metering port in the hydraulic head.

End plate and regulating valve

The end plate houses the regulating valve assembly and a fine mesh nylon filter. The fuel inlet connection which locates and secures this assembly is mounted externally.

A beautifully restored MF 35X Multi-Power from the Coldridge collection. It is coupled to a Massey Ferguson trailed spinner.

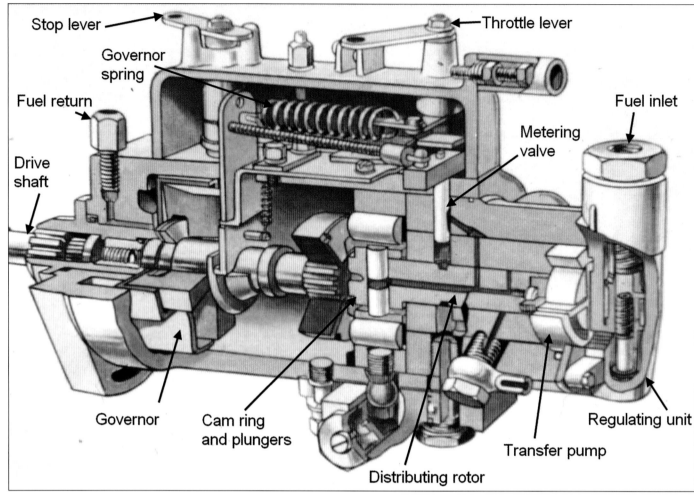

Stop lever — Throttle lever
Governor spring
Fuel return — Fuel inlet
Drive shaft — Metering valve
Governor — Cam ring and plungers — Distributing rotor — Transfer pump — Regulating unit

6.71. DPA pump

The regulating valve performs two separate functions. Firstly, it controls transfer pressure, maintaining a predetermined relationship between the pressure and the speed of rotation. Secondly, it provides a means of bypassing the vanes of the transfer pump when the pump is stationary, so that the fuel passages in the hydraulic head can be primed.

Fuel entering the end plate at feed pressure passes to the inlet side of the transfer pump through the nylon filter and the upper fuel passage.

Transfer pressure is transmitted to the underside of the regulating piston through the lower fuel passage and tends to force the piston upwards. This force is opposed by pressure exerted on the upper face of the piston by the regulating spring.

As transfer pressure rises with increasing engine speed the piston is forced upwards and the regulating spring is compressed. Such movement of the piston progressively uncovers the regulating port and regulates transfer pressure by permitting a metered flow of fuel back to the inlet side of the transfer pump. The effective area of the regulating port is increased as engine speed is raised, and is reduced as engine speed falls.

When priming a pump, fuel entering the end plate cannot pass through the transfer pump and into the fuel passages in the hydraulic head in the normal way. Fuel at priming pressure enters the valve sleeve and acts on the upper face of the regulating piston. The piston is forced to the lower end of the valve sleeve, compressing the priming spring and uncovering the priming

ports. Fuel passes through the priming ports and the lower fuel passage to the outlet side of the transfer pump, and then into the fuel passages within the hydraulic head.

Maximum fuel adjustment

Since the amount of outward displacement of the plungers is governed by the amount of fuel permitted to enter the element, a maximum fuel setting can be made by limiting the maximum outward movement of the plungers. This setting is made after manufacture or overhaul and must not be altered by the operator.

The numbers stamped on the type plate attached to the pump housing identify the type and model of the pump. Pumps that are of identical build,

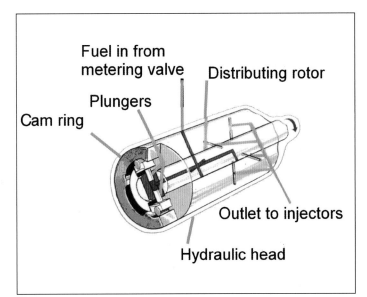

6.72. Internal of DPA injection pump

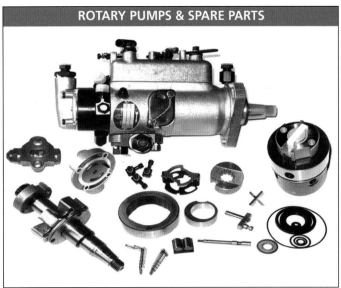

ROTARY PUMPS & SPARE PARTS

6.73. DPA injection pump spare parts

but set differently to suit different applications are further identified by the setting code stamped beneath the ordering number. Note: should the pump need to be replaced the codes must match for the engine to work correctly.

6.71. The main features can be seen in the cutaway illustration. There is a central rotating steel member known as the pumping and distributing rotor; this is driven by splines from a drive shaft via the engine timing gear, or chain, and carries at its outer end a vane-type fuel transfer pump. The rotor is a close fit in a stationary steel cylindrical body, called the hydraulic head. The pumping section of the rotor has a transverse bore containing two opposed pump plungers. These rotate inside a cam ring in the pump housing, and operate through rollers and shoes sliding in the rotor. The cam ring has as many internal lobes as the engine has cylinders (i.e. 3 or 4). The opposed plungers have no springs, but are moved outwards by fuel pressure.

The distributing part of the rotor contains a central axial passage that connects the pumping space between the plungers with ports drilled radially in the rotor. One radial hole is the distributing port, and as the rotor turns it aligns successively with a number of outlet ports (equal to the number of engine cylinders) in the hydraulic head, from

which the injectors are fed via external high-pressure pipes. A similar number of inlet ports in the rotor align successively with a single port in the head. This is the inlet or metering port, and it admits fuel under the control of the governor.

6.72. Pumping and distribution of the metered fuel is determined by the internal rotor. As the rotor turns, a charging port is aligned with the metering port in the hydraulic head and fuel at metered pressure flows into the central passage in the rotor and forces the plungers apart. The amount of plunger displacement is determined by the amount of fuel that can flow into the element while the ports are aligned.

The inlet port closes as rotation continues, and as the single distributor port in the rotor comes into alignment with one of the distributor ports in the hydraulic head, the actuating rollers contact the cam ring lobes and the plungers are forced inwards. High pressure, between 120 and 130 bar (1,740 and 1,886 psi), is generated and fuel passes to the injector.

6.73. In front of a distributor pump type A (DPA) fuel injection pump are the typical internal parts which will need to be replaced if the fuel has been contaminated by dirt, water or poorly made biodiesel – not to mention general wear and tear. These internal parts are minute and require clean fuel to lubricate them.

Chapter 7 | Transmissions

The transmission fitted to the Massey Ferguson 35 tractor can be either single clutch as fitted to the 'basic' model tractor or a dual clutch fitted to the deluxe version of the tractor. Either model can be fitted with a mechanical sliding mesh six speed, an option from 1962 or a 'change on the move' Multi-Power gearbox. The Multi-Power enables the operator to change the gearbox speed/ratio with the flick of a switch mounted on the right-hand side of the dash.

3-Cylinder Engine Clutch Repair

In the past you could strip down and repair the individual parts of a clutch, but as the price of the complete unit has dropped it is easier and less time consuming to use a new double or dual clutch assembly. This is available as a kit including new friction plates, thrust and pilot (or spigot) bearings. It is a ready-to-fit unit which is pre-set at the factory and does not require any adjustments to be carried out, although you will require a centre clutch aligning tool. This can be produced from a ½ in drive, long extension bar and insulation tape but you could machine one in metal or wood from the dimensions given in the photograph on page 117 for more accuracy. The alternative to fitting a complete new assembly would be to strip down and recondition the old clutch unit. It is necessary to separate the clutch because the PTO plate is captive within the middle of the clutch cover. Reconditioning is a good option if you have the time or if the clutch assembly only requires new friction plates. Using extreme care, it is possible to save money by dismantling and overhauling the clutch in individual pieces.

The transmission clutch on agricultural tractors comes in two versions. The single-clutch transmission has one friction plate that drives just the rear wheels, while the double-clutch transmission has two friction plates that drive both the rear wheels and the PTO gears independently. Both clutches serve the same purposes: to engage and disengage the drive to the wheels or PTO, to give a progressive smooth engagement, to provide positive 1:1 drive and to transmit high torque at varying engine speeds.

Common clutch faults are listed in the table opposite, along with the recommended remedies; these will usually work on either version of clutch. Unfortunately in most cases it will be necessary to split the tractor at the clutch (bell) housing to investigate the problems with the clutch unit.

7.01. Mass clutch change

The following pictures indicate faults and provide tips for working on the clutch unit. Be very careful when removing the dual clutch assembly from the flywheel. **Note: All Massey Ferguson tractors require slave or captive bolts (¼ UNC x 2¼) to be fitted to restrain the spring pressure before removing the clutch from the flywheel.** Please seek advice from a knowledgeable person before attempting to remove the clutch.

7.01. Tractor clutch changing can be carried out with the help of two or three people. It is preferable to use two trolley jacks and axle stands for safety. Wooden wedges need to be fitted between the front axle beam and axle centre casing to prevent the engine tipping to one side when separated from the gearbox. Clamps can be used to lock the drag link and radius arms into the straight-ahead position for the front wheels. This makes it easier to move the tractor forwards and backwards when servicing.

7.02. With the new clutch fitted, the pedal free play – the clearance between the upper side of the pedal and the underside of the foot rest bracket – will need to be adjusted. This is achieved by slackening the pinch bolt, placing a bar

CLUTCH FAULT	FAULT	REMEDY
Slip – The most common fault. With the engine running the revs will increase and there is little or no forward movement; this will possibly be accompanied by a burning smell. Continued use will lead to overheating and damage to the clutch and flywheel faces. Heat will soften the clutch springs, leading to further slippage.	No clutch pedal free play.	Check and adjust.
	Oil on friction plates.	Cure the leak and replace the linings.
	Binding of clutch controls.	Oil, adjust or repair.
	Worn out clutch plates.	Replace assembly.
	Weak clutch springs.	Replace springs (in sets).
Judder – When the clutch is being engaged from a stationary position and the tractor moves off in sudden jerks.	Operator.	Learn to drive!
	Loose gearbox bolts.	Check and tighten.
	Oil, grease or other liquid (water) on the linings.	Check, clean or replace.
	Warped clutch plate.	Replace.
	Loose or broken clutch linings.	Check and replace.
	Worn thrust bearing.	Check and replace.
	Broken or weak pressure springs.	Check and replace.
Snatch – This happens when the clutch is engaged, the drive take up is severe and the tractor lurches forward.	See Judder.	See Judder.
	Broken or worn cushion springs and splines.	Check and replace.
Rattle – This is a continuous noise from the clutch area when the engine is running, whether in or out of gear. *N.B. Excessive wear in the transmission will cause a vibration along the clutch shaft causing a rattle or noise to appear to be coming from the clutch housing.*	Caused by the following worn or broken parts: toggle fingers, springs, pilot bearing, thrust bearing.	If the noise stops with the clutch pedal depressed then the bearing is worn.
Drag – Two possible scenarios. One, when the clutch pedal is fully depressed the tractor may still move forward. Two, the gears are difficult to engage and disengage because the input shaft to the gearbox is still driven.	Too much pedal free play.	Check and adjust.
	Oil on friction plates.	Clean or fit new.
	Pedal bent or mud under it.	Check and/or clean.
	Worn or rusty splines on the input shaft.	Renew or lubricate.
	Seized pilot bearing.	Check and replace.
	Worn thrust bearing.	Check and replace.
	Distorted or broken drive plate. (This could be due to poor refitment.)	Check and replace.
	Warped pressure plate and clutch cover.	Check and replace.
	Toggle fingers and linkage broken or worn out.	Check and replace.

in the hole provided and moving the pedal to give the correct free play. Then you must re-tighten the pinch bolt. If there is too much clearance the PTO clutch will not be fully disengaged and the PTO lever will be difficult to select.

7.03. This picture illustrates the layout and orientation of the parts of a double clutch. Note that the Belleville spring must face up towards the clutch cover. The springs are colour coded: yellow in this clutch indicates the strength or poundage to transmit the torque of the engine. If fitting new springs make sure they are the same colour. It is possible if the tractor is fitted with a loader to increase the spring pressure, and therefore clutch 'bite', by fitting stronger springs. It is worth noting that

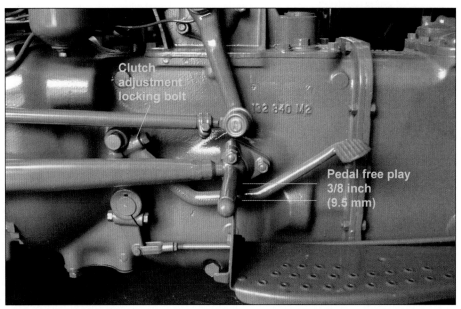

7.02. Clutch pedal free play

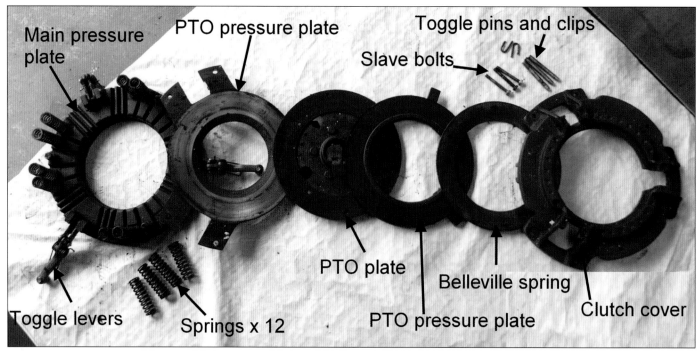

7.03. MF double clutch layout

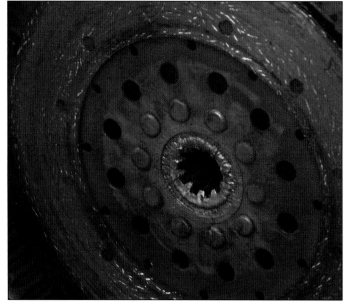

7.04. Worn-out friction plate

some new clutches have been updated and do not have coil springs as these have been replaced by Belleville springs.

7.04. By investigating the degree of wear and amount of oil on the main friction plate, you can determine what is causing a lack of drive on a warmed-up tractor. Note how close the rivets are to the friction material; this indicates a very worn surface. As the plate wears, the springs cannot exert the same amount of pressure on the plate; therefore, the clutch will slip and the wear rate will increase rapidly.

7.05. Two faults have occurred with this clutch, even though it appears to be quite new (as evidenced by the fact that the

7.05. Oil contamination

7.06. Scored pressure plate

7.07. Friction materials

7.08. Glazed friction plate

7.09. Rusted plate and spacers

maker's name is still visible on the friction surface). The oil leak which affected the original clutch was not fixed which means that the leak contaminated the new friction plates again. The oil is clear brown in colour, which suggests that it is probably coming from the gearbox. The small piece of cast is from the broken clutch cover; this could be because of poor reassembly of the cover or because it has been incorrectly fitted to the tractor.

7.06. If the friction plate material wears down and exposes the securing rivets, then scoring of the flywheel and the clutch cover pressure plate surfaces will occur. This will necessitate the replacement of the cover and machining of the flywheel.

7.07. Two types of friction material could be used on the tractor clutch plates. On older tractors asbestos was commonly used but was discontinued in the 1980s because it was deemed a health risk. Be careful when replacing the clutch, it could be fitted with the older type in which case you should make sure to keep the dust dampened down. The other clutch is a heavy-duty sintered paddle clutch. The number of plates is determined by the torque of the tractor's engine – more plates allow more power to be transmitted through the clutch. These clutches are hard and because of this they often score the flywheel and the clutch pressure plate.

7.08. Oil and continued clutch operation can glaze the surface of the clutch leading to judder and snatching when taking up

7.10. Dusty bell housing, noisy thrust

the drive. Uneven markings indicate that the clutch has not been engaged evenly.

7.09. If the tractor is not used for long periods, it is advisable to lock down the clutch pedal in the disengaged position. This will prevent moisture from sticking the friction plate to the flywheel. MF 35 tractors have a lever fitted to the front of the foot plate for this purpose. The three spacer washers are used to aid cooling and provide the correct height for the toggle operating levers.

7.10. Oil on the main clutch friction plate will be evident and any traces must be removed with a clutch/brake cleaner or similar fluid. Again, beware of asbestos being used as the

7.11. Oil from gearbox

7.12. Pilot bearing

7.13. Springs and heat scoring

frictional material. Keep down the dust when cleaning by dampening with fluid – do not use an air jet – and make sure to dispose of the old unit thoughtfully. As a matter of course, the thrust bearing was replaced because it was loose and noisy.

7.11. Although the clutch cover and friction plates are new, the oil leak from the gearbox has rendered them useless. It is relatively easy to determine the origin of any oil leak: black oil is from the engine and clean or slightly brown oil will be from the transmission.

7.12. When you renew the clutch assembly it is logical to replace the pilot or spigot bearing to ensure reliability. As the bearing wears it runs the risk of seizing up and if it does seize, then it will cause clutch and gearbox engagement problems. With the flywheel off, the bearing can be easily removed by tapping it out from the engine side. A new one can then be pressed in.

7.13. The scoring on the PTO pressure plate can be seen as dark or blue markings; it has also caused crazing, or cracking, of the plate. If reusing the old clutch, check that the springs have not been heated; they should still have the colour coding on them. They will need to be compared against each other and must all measure the same height. If replacing the springs ensure you fit new heat washers underneath them.

7.14. Worn toggle lever buttons

7.14. The toggle levers are contacted by the thrust bearing and their job is to disengage and engage the clutch. If there is a lack of pedal clearance or the operator holds his/her foot on the clutch pedal, then the buttons on the ends will wear and the friction plates will slip.

7.15. After fitting the slave bolts to the cover and removing the clutch from the tractor it is then fitted into a hydraulic press. A bar is fitted on top of the clutch and hydraulic pressure is used to compress the clutch springs. The slave bolts and toggle lever pins can be removed and the hydraulic pressure can be released.

7.16. An alternative to using a hydraulic press is to fit longer slave bolts to the clutch with nuts attached. These can then be used to compress the clutch spring pressure. Once the clutch is removed from the flywheel the nuts can be slackened off evenly and the clutch spring pressure released to enable the unit to be stripped down and inspected or the PTO friction plate replaced.

7.16. Slave bolts to strip clutch

7.17. Using alignment tool

7.15. Hydraulic press

PTO
Clearance
tool 0.090
inch (2.3mm)

Release lever height tool

52.45 mm

230.00 mm

16.88   22.98   37.92

21.40   53.70 mm   40.00 mm

**Friction plate
alignment tool**

7.18. Clutch tools

7.17. When aligning the main drive and PTO drive friction plates centrally with the pilot or spigot bearing, a tool can be made from metal or wood to enable ease of fitment to the gearbox input shafts.

7.18. Dimensions of the clutch tools required when using the old clutch cover and fitting new friction plates. These tools are sufficient for fitting Massey Ferguson double clutches on both petrol and diesel 3- and 4-cylinder engines.

7.19. Before fitting a new clutch friction plate it is advisable to check that the splines on the plate will fit the input shafts of the gearbox. It is not uncommon to be supplied with the wrong part. These must be checked before fitting on the input shaft otherwise the gearbox will not fit back onto the engine.

7.19. Check new against old

4-Cylinder Engine Double Clutch and Flywheel Overhaul

🔧 Tools required for checks:

Range of imperial spanners and ⅜ and ½ sockets

Torque wrench

Clutch aligning tool

Clutch release level tool

PTO clearance tool

Lifting crane and straps

Hammer and a small chisel

Wire brushes and air drill

Locking wire

The dual clutch fitted to the Massey Ferguson 35 tractor varies from the single clutch 'basic' version in that it incorporates two friction plates operated via a single clutch pedal. The first downward movement of the pedal disconnects the drive to the rear wheels, and the final 25 mm (1 in) of pedal travel disconnects the drive to the PTO and hydraulic system. This enables the PTO drive to a machine to be continuously operated but still allows the tractor to stop or change gear ratio.

The dual clutch comprises two friction plates. The main drive measures 279 mm (11 in) in diameter and the PTO measures 229 mm (9 in) in diameter. Accessing the clutch assembly is the same procedure as the single clutch; the only variations concern the type of engine fitted as different parts will need to be disconnected to permit different engines to be separated from the gearbox.

Overhauling the dual clutch

To overhaul the dual clutch assembly follow the pictorial procedure:

7.20. Check that the starter motor flywheel ring gear teeth are in good condition. As with any engine it will stop in one of two positions and therefore wear the teeth more in this area. If the teeth are worn, inspect the condition of the starter motor pinion teeth. To remove the flywheel ring gear it is necessary to drill an 8 mm (⁵⁄₁₆ in) hole as near as possible to the inside edge of the ring. Using a cold chisel, split the hole open to release the ring gear from the flywheel. Note: the leading edge of the ring has been worn away.

7.21. To fit the new ring gear to the flywheel, first ensure the leading tapered edge of the ring gear is facing the front of the tractor. Gently and evenly heat the ring gear until it expands enough to drop into position on the flywheel. Tap into place using a hammer and taper punch. Do not heat the ring gear too much as this will affect its hardness and will cause it to wear very quickly.

7.20. Removing ring gear

7.21. Fitting ring gear

7.22. Torque flywheel bolts

7.23. Release lever height setting

7.24. PTO clutch clearance

7.25. Friction plate alignment tool

7.26. Thrust bearing parts

lever height using the bridging tool as shown. You should do this to ensure all are at the same height from the flywheel. Any adjustment is carried out by slackening the lock nut and turning the slotted screw on each lever.

7.24. The PTO friction plate clearance adjustment is set to 2.3 mm (0.090 in) using the setting tool or feeler gauges. Slacken the lock nut and adjust the screw to the required clearance.

7.25. When aligning the main drive and PTO drive friction plates centrally with the pilot or spigot bearing, a tool can be made from metal or wood to enable ease of fitment to the gearbox input shafts.

7.26. The thrust clutch release bearing contacts with the release levers to engage and disengage the clutch friction plates. It makes sense to replace the bearing and the carrier if it is worn when the tractor is split for a clutch overhaul. The new bearing should be pressed onto the new carrier using a hydraulic press or large vice, not hammered on as this can damage the parts. Note the locking screws are prevented from loosening by the use of locking wire fitted through the holes in the top of these screws.

7.22. Fit the new pilot or spigot bearing into the flywheel and, using the small locating hole, fit the flywheel to the crankshaft. Apply a thread locking compound to the flywheel bolts and torque to 124–138 Nm (90–100 lb-ft).

Using a dial test indicator, check that the friction surface face run out is 0.762 mm (0.003 in) and if it is outside these figures check the flywheel to crankshaft mounting flange for dirt or burrs. If it is within the limits bend over the locking tabs.

7.23. If using the old clutch cover and fitting a new friction plate you will need to check and adjust the toggle or release

7.27. Check friction plate orientation

7.28. Using alignment tool

7.29. Refitting engine to gearbox

7.27. When fitting the new main friction plate ensure the marked 'flywheel side' is positioned correctly and the three shims are positioned on the rim of the clutch cover.

7.28. Using the friction plate alignment tool fit the clutch to the flywheel. Then tighten the six bolts evenly to 30–33 Nm (22–24 lb-ft). Check that the tool slides easily in and out of the clutch confirming that the shafts are aligned correctly.

7.29. Apply copper grease to the gearbox input splines and the thrust bearing housing. Using tapered dowels screwed into the gearbox to ease housing alignment, fit the engine to the gearbox ensuring the gap/housing edges are parallel. Turn the engine using the fan blades. Ensure the gear levers are engaged in order to align the input shaft splines. Turn the PTO shaft at the rear of the tractor to engage the input shaft. Then tighten the bell housing bolts to 69–76 Nm (50–55 lb-ft).

7.30. With the new clutch fitted, the pedal free play will need to be adjusted. The free play refers to the clearance between the upper side of the pedal and the under side of the foot rest bracket. Adjustment is achieved by slackening the pinch bolt, setting the free play using a bar in the hole provided and then tightening the pinch bolt.

7.31. For clutch tools see picture 7.18.

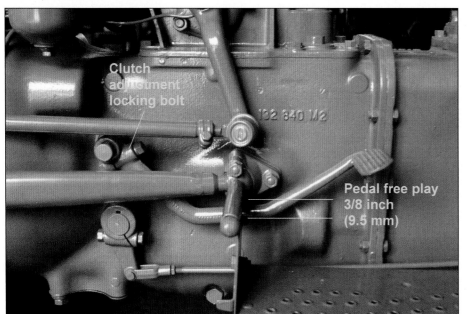

Clutch adjustment locking bolt

Pedal free play 3/8 inch (9.5 mm)

7.30. Clutch pedal free play

Single Clutch and Flywheel Overhaul

The tractor serial number can be used to confirm the type of clutch fitted to a particular tractor. (See Chapter 1 – Buying and Safety on page 11.) Single plate units used on the 'basic' model tractors have a 229 mm (9 in) Petrol/TVO engine or 254 mm (10 in) diesel engine diameter friction plate. They do not have a separate drive for the PTO and therefore when the clutch pedal is depressed the PTO, hydraulics and rear linkage arms will stop working.

If a clutch is found to be slipping, it could be because the friction plates are worn out or there is a lack of pedal free play. If, on the other hand, oil is evident from the bottom of the bell housing (the front of the gearbox), then you should look at the colour of the oil as this will indicate the source of the leak. Black oil indicates that the leak is from the engine, while clear is a gearbox oil leakage. (See dual clutch fault chart on page 113.)

Oil on the main clutch friction plate will easily be evident and any traces must be removed with a clutch/brake cleaner or similar fluid. Beware that some older clutch frictional materials may be made from asbestos; keep dust dampened down when cleaning. Do not use a compressed air jet to blow away any dust!

The flywheel is a very heavy unit so be careful when removing from the engine. At the same time, be sure to note the

🔧 Tools required for checks:

Range of imperial spanners and ⅜ and ½ sockets	Lifting crane and straps
	Hammer and a small chisel
Torque wrench	Wire brushes and air drill
Clutch aligning tool	Locking wire

alignment hole, which is used to ensure the timing marks on the flywheel are in the correct position. Any scoring or cracks on the friction surface of the flywheel is caused by leaving it too long before replacement of the friction plate. Clutch slippage leads to a heat build-up that wears the friction plate material away. This causes rivets to contact the flywheel and wear grooves in the surface. The surface will need to be machined by a local engineering company; alternatively, if the wear is too excessive a replacement flywheel will be necessary.

Check that the starter motor flywheel ring gear teeth are in good condition. As with any engine it will stop in one of two positions and therefore wear the teeth more in this area. Further, if the teeth are worn, inspect the condition of the starter motor pinion teeth.

A new clutch assembly is delivered pre-set and can be fitted without any adjustments. The pictures demonstrate the procedures required if reusing the old clutch parts with new friction plates fitted.

To overhaul the clutch assembly follow the pictorial procedure:

7.32. With the new clutch fitted, the pedal free play – the clearance between the upper side of the pedal and the underside of the foot rest bracket – will need to be adjusted. This is achieved by slackening the pinch bolt, placing a bar in the hole provided and moving the pedal to give the correct free play. Then you must re-tighten the pinch bolt.

7.33. With the bonnet and fuel tank removed and the wiring (together with the fuel lines) disconnected, the tractor can be split at the transmission bell housing at the rear of the engine. Conveniently, the engine is fitted with lifting eyes which permit a balanced attachment of the shackles and a lifting strop. Alternatively, trolley jacks and axle stands could be used. Ensure wooden wedges are fitted on either side of the front axle (between the front casing) to lock it into place to prevent the engine tipping to one side when it is removed from the gearbox.

7.32. Clutch pedal free play

7.33. Engine separated

7.34. Remove single clutch

7.35. Replace spigot bearing

7.36. Line up flywheel

7.37. Fit new plate

7.38. Using alignment tool

7.34. Slacken off the six bolts evenly securing the clutch cover to the flywheel. The cover and friction plate can then be lifted off. Mark the friction plate to enable it to be refitted in the correct orientation if being reused. Inspect the cover and flywheel surfaces for scoring and heat cracking, check for oil contamination and make the necessary repairs.

7.35. The pilot or spigot bearing should be replaced as a matter of course to ensure its reliability. If the bearing seizes, it will cause clutch and gearbox engagement problems. The bearing can be easily removed with the flywheel off by tapping it out from the engine side. Once it is out a new one can then be pressed in.

7.39. Bell housing

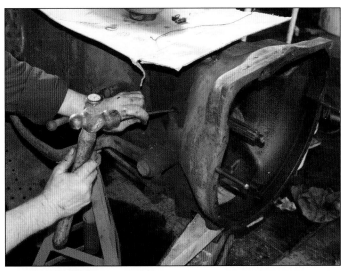

7.40. Replace bushes

7.41. Thrust bearing, single clutch

7.36. Using the small locating hole, fit the flywheel to the crankshaft. Apply a thread locking compound to the flywheel bolts and torque to 124–138 Nm (90–100 lb-ft). Using a dial test indicator, check that the friction surface face run out is 0.762 mm (0.003 in); if it is outside these measurements, then check the flywheel to crankshaft mounting flange for dirt or burrs. If it is within limits, bend over the locking tabs.

7.37. When fitting the new main friction plate ensure the marked 'flywheel side' is positioned correctly. To aid alignment of the input shaft and the friction plate you can make a dummy alignment tool using a long half drive extension bar or by fabricating one from metal or wood. This will enable ease of fitment to the gearbox input shaft. Note: universal alignment tools are available from tool suppliers.

7.38. Use the friction plate alignment tool to fit the clutch to the flywheel. Then torque the six bolts evenly to 30–33 Nm (22–24 lb-ft). Check that the tool slides easily in and out of the clutch; this confirms that the shafts are aligned correctly.

7.39. Excessive play on the clutch shaft, which the pedal attaches to, can be attributed to worn bushes within the gearbox casing.

7.42. Refit engine

To remove the shafts, first cut the locking wire that is fitted through the holes in the top of the square-head screws. Remove the screws and tap out the shafts.

7.40. Remove the worn bushes using a small chisel. Then gently tap the new bushes into the housing.

7.41. The thrust clutch release bearing contacts with the release levers to engage and disengage the clutch friction plates. If the bearing and the carrier are worn, then it makes sense to replace them when the tractor is split for a clutch overhaul.

The new bearing should be pressed onto the new carrier using a hydraulic press or large vice. Do not hammer on the bearing as this can damage the parts.

7.42. Apply copper grease to the gearbox input splines and the thrust bearing housing. Using tapered dowels screwed into the gearbox to ease housing alignment, fit the engine to the gearbox ensuring the gap or housing machined edges are parallel. Then turn the engine using the fan blades. Ensure the gear levers are engaged in order to align the input shaft splines. Tighten the bell housing bolts to 69–76 Nm (50–55 lb-ft).

Six-Speed Gearbox Overhaul

🔧 **Tools required for checks:**

Range of imperial spanners and ⅜ and ½ sockets
Torque wrench
Lifting crane and straps
Hammer and a small chisel
Circlip and 'C' clip pliers
Locking wire
Oil seal removing tool
Oil seal dolly
Small magnet

The Massey Ferguson 35 tractor standard transmission is fitted with a three forward and one reverse gearbox with an epicyclic high/low reduction unit to the rear of the gearbox housing enabling double the output gears, e.g. six forward and two reverse.

When dismantling any gearbox it is imperative to have a manual to hand or someone who has experience of dismantling the particular gearbox, as the procedures vary with each transmission. Some gearboxes require special tools and equipment for resetting the components on reassembly. Fortunately the MF gearbox only requires circlips and special 'C' clip pliers to remove the gear and bearing retaining clips; these can be obtained from any good tool supplier.

A methodical approach to stripping the gearbox is very important and keeping the parts in order of disassembly will cause less head scratching on the rebuilding of the transmission. Either mark the parts with correction fluid or if possible use string to link them as they are removed from the gearbox housing. To access the gearbox it is necessary to remove the dash panel, wiring and fuel lines together with the steering box, which incorporates the two gear levers. First remove the drag link joints at the bottom of the steering box arms beforehand. The brake linkages going to the rear of the tractor are disconnected at the gearbox and the radius rods disconnected from their sockets on either side of the gearbox casing. Then the gearbox can be unbolted from the rear of the engine and the front of the rear axle casing. The use of lifting straps and a small crane is advisable because of the weight of the gearbox assembly. Place it on a sturdy bench ideally with a wooden surface to prevent slippage and use wooden wedges to secure it in place.

With the gearbox dismantled inspect the gear teeth for pitting, scoring or missing parts! Check the bearings for smooth running and little side play. Any suspect parts should be replaced to ensure reliability.

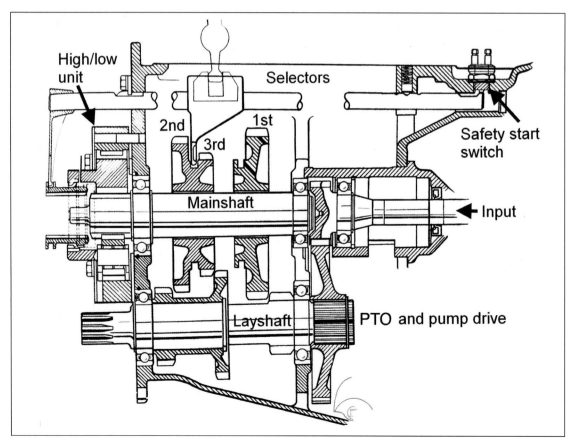

7.43. This is the layout of the component parts of the single-clutch gearbox. Note that the drive to the gearbox and the PTO/hydraulic pump is determined by the clutch engagement. The Multi-Power gearbox (on page 132) demonstrates the drive through the dual clutch transmission.

7.43. MF 35 six-speed gearbox

To overhaul the six-speed gearbox follow the pictorial procedure:

7.44. Remove steering box

7.45. View of gearbox top

7.46. Remove rear high/low unit

7.44. The first task in dismantling the gearbox is to remove the steering box which forms the top of the gearbox and also houses the two gear levers. Take care once the steering drag link arms have been removed from the steering box drop arms as it is possible to accidently spin the steering wheel, which would cause the internal steering shaft to unwind completely. To prevent this it is advisable to tie the steering wheel to the throttle lever.

7.45. This is the sight that will greet you once you have removed the top cover. After draining the oil from the plug at the lowest

7.47. Remove selector rails

part of the gearbox casing, you will usually be able to see any damaged gears.

7.46. To dismantle the six-speed gearbox, first remove the rear high/low reduction unit. Remove the two bolts at the top of the rear casing: these hold the interlock unit which will only allow one gear to be selected at a time.

Slide out the high/low selector rail, turning it through 90 degrees, and unbolt the gear lever coupling on the shaft inside the gearbox. Fully withdraw the selector shaft and unbolt the high/low reduction unit keeping the parts together for inspection later.

7.47. The main gear selector rails can be withdrawn one at a time after cutting off the locking wires. The gear lever couplings can then be refitted as the rails are withdrawn. This enables the correct orientation and eases reassembly. If in any doubt use masking tape secured to each rail.

7.48. The three detents at the front of the gearbox lock or hold the selected gear into position; this prevents it jumping out of gear. Obviously if your gearbox does jump out of gear, then you will need to replace the detents, springs and/or the selector rails.

7.48. Remove detents

7.49. Lower shaft cover

7.50. Remove input shaft

7.51. Remove top shaft

Use a small magnet to withdraw the detents from the gearbox casing. (Maximum spring length is 26.19 mm, or 1 $\frac{1}{32}$ in.)

7.49. Remove the clutch operating linkage. Unbolt the left-hand-side brake linkage, remove the arm and key and slide the shaft out from the right-hand side. Remove the lower round cover and snap ring and, using two slave set bolts ($\frac{9}{16}$ x 3 in UNC), withdraw the bearing housing. Remove the thrust washer, noting that the raised edge faces toward the front.

7.50. Remove the lower snap ring from the PTO shaft and gently tap it forwards using a soft-faced copper hammer. This will allow the drive gear to drop down and enable the top input shaft housing to be withdrawn when the four bolts are removed.

7.51. Remove the snap ring from the front of the top shaft and gently tap the shaft towards the rear using a wooden dowel. Lift out the front bearing and slide the top shaft out of the three gears noting their orientation. The gears can now be removed from the gearbox.

7.52. Remove reverse idler

7.52. Unbolt and remove the rear locating plate at the back of the gearbox and slide out the reverse idler shaft. Lift the reverse gear out with the needle roller bearing attached inside.

7.53. Before removing the lay (lower) shaft, you will have to first take off the snap ring from the front of the helical cut (constant mesh) gear. Remove the snap ring from the rear bearing and drive the shaft towards the front of the gearbox. Then remove the lower gears.

7.54. Before fitting the lay shaft it is easier to assemble the reverse idler gear, spacers and needle bearings with Vaseline or similar grease to hold them all into position. Then slide the support shaft into the gearbox housing, taking care not to disturb the rollers. Refitting the lay shaft means tapping the shaft far enough towards the rear of the gearbox so that the lower two gears can slide onto the shaft. Ensure the two large hubs on the gears face each other and that the larger of the two gears is fitted to the front of the gearbox.

7.55. Fitting the main shaft is basically a reversal of the strip down but you will need to fit new 'C' clips as the old ones will stretch out of shape when they are removed. Ensure the gears are refitted as per the picture.

7.53. Lay shaft gear layout

7.54. Refit lay shaft

7.55. Main shaft refit

7.56. Main input seal removed

7.56. The input shaft housing is stripped down after removing the large 'C' clip from the rear of the housing by tapping the shaft gently on a wooden surface. The inner seal can be removed with a seal 'hook' tool.

7.57. Refit new input seal

7.57. The new input shaft seal should be refitted with a dolly made from a suitably sized solid metal bar.

7.58. Fit new PTO seal

7.59. Shaft splines protected

7.60. Rebuilt housing

7.61. Constant mesh gears

7.58. Fit the PTO input shaft seal using a socket that is just slightly smaller than the seal diameter. Gently tap the seal into position.

7.59. To prevent damage to the new seals, wrap masking tape around the shaft splines, oil them and then slide the components together.

7.60. Gently tap the input (inner) shaft into the housing and locate the large circlip into the groove in the inner housing.

7.61. Slide the rear helical cut (constant mesh) gear onto the lay shaft and secure with a new 'C' clip. Lower the front helical cut gear into the front of the gearbox case with the hubs on the gears positioned as shown.

7.62. Refit PTO input shaft

7.62. This is the layout of the front constant mesh gear, PTO shaft and front bearing support housing.

7.63. Obtain or make a new input shaft housing gasket and refit it into the front of the gearbox bell (clutch) housing. Slide the PTO shaft in from the front of the gearbox and

7.63. Make new gasket

fit a new 'C' clip. Refit the thrust washer with the raised lip facing forwards.

Using a piece of wood at the rear of the PTO shaft, hold in position and gently tap the front bearing and housing into place. Fit the front cover with a new gasket.

7.64. Refit detents

7.65. High/low unit layout

7.66. Fit locking wire

7.67. Ream brake shaft bushes

7.68. Completed gearbox

7.64. Refit the selector rails and gear lever couplings, ensuring they are in the correct positions as shown. Refit the detents and springs.

7.65. Replace any worn gears or shim plates in the epicyclic high/low unit and refit in the order shown. The left-hand side fits to the rear of the gearbox casing first.

7.66. Tighten the square-headed locking screw on the selector rail gear lever coupling. Soft flexible (16 Standard Wire Gauge) locking wire is used to hold the screw securely in position. Refit the gear lever interlock unit between the selector rails.

7.67. Before fitting the brake shaft the old bushes are removed and new ones fitted. The new ones will need to be reamed to the correct size to fit the brake shaft. Once that is done, refit the clutch thrust bearing housing and shafts, securing the square-headed screws with locking wire.

7.68. After ensuring the gear levers are not worn and do not have excessive play in the housing pivots, you can refit the steering box. Fit a new top gasket and when lowering the steering box ensure the two levers locate into the selector rail couplings.

Multi-Power Gearbox Overhaul

🔧 Tools required for checks:

Range of imperial spanners and ⅜ and ½ sockets	Circlip and 'C' clip pliers
	Locking wire
Torque wrench	Oil seal removing tool
Lifting crane and straps	Oil seal dolly
Hammer and a small chisel	Small magnet
	Seal puller

A Multi-Power gearbox is fitted with a standard mechanical three forward and one reverse gearbox with an epicyclic high/low reduction unit to the rear of the gearbox housing enabling double the output gears, e.g. six forward and two reverse. In conjunction, an extra pair of gears at the front of the gearbox – selected by the Multi-Power clutch pack – enables the operator to 'change on the move'. The driver is also able to under load one gear by the use of a lever mounted on the dash. The gearbox then becomes a twelve forward and four reverse transmission. Unfortunately because of the use of a one-way dog clutch – to enable the constant mesh Multi-Power gears to work – if the tractor is used on sloping ground in low Multi-Power range, the dog clutch will work in the opposite position. It will disengage the drive and there will be no engine braking to slow down the tractor. (You only do this once!)

When dismantling any gearbox it is imperative to have a manual to hand or someone who has experience of dismantling the particular gearbox because the procedures vary with each transmission. The MF gearbox only requires circlips and special 'C' clip pliers to remove the gear and bearing retaining clips. When repairing the Multi-Power piston rings and seals located on the input shafts it is important to take care as the parts are delicate.

A methodical approach to stripping the gearbox is very important and keeping the parts in order of disassembly will caused less head scratching on the rebuilding of the transmission. Either mark the parts with correction fluid or, if possible, use string to link them as they are removed from the gearbox

housing. To access the gearbox it is necessary to remove the dash panel, wiring and fuel lines together with the steering box, which incorporates the two gear levers. Remove the drag link joints at the bottom of the steering box arms beforehand. The brake linkages going to the rear of the tractor are disconnected at the gearbox and the radius rods are disconnected from their sockets on either side of the gearbox casing. After disconnecting the Multi-Power internal pipe, the gearbox can be unbolted from the rear of the engine and the front of the rear axle casing. It is advisable to use lifting straps and a small crane to remove the gearbox because of the weight of the gearbox assembly. Place it on a sturdy bench, ideally with a wooden surface to prevent slippage, and use wooden wedges to secure it in place.

With the gearbox dismantled inspect the gear teeth for pitting and/or scoring. Check the bearings for smooth running and any side play. The Multi-Power components inspection and repair are explained in detail in the pictures. Any suspect parts should be replaced to ensure reliability. Note that some parts for the Multi-Power – e.g. the hydraulic oil pump and input shaft housing – are now becoming difficult to obtain because of the low number of tractors produced with this gearbox.

7.69. Multi-Power test

7.70. Multi-Power test number two

7.69. This tractor is fitted with a Multi-Power change on the move high and low gearbox and must be checked for correct operation. Test 1 is carried out on an incline, the tractor is driven up the hill in Multi-Power 'high' and then the clutch depressed, as the tractor rolls backwards the transmission dog clutch and clutch pack should 'lock up' and stop the tractor. This confirms that the Multi-Power components are functioning correctly.

7.70. Test 2 involves driving the tractor at various speeds and on differing inclines and checking that the Multi-Power lever selects and de-selects high and low firmly and positively. To get the engine and transmission oil at working temperature, drive for at least two miles or one hour. Then carry out test 1 again before finishing the drive.

7.71. This is the layout of the Multi-Power gearbox. The front section houses the Multi-Power clutch pack, dog clutch and

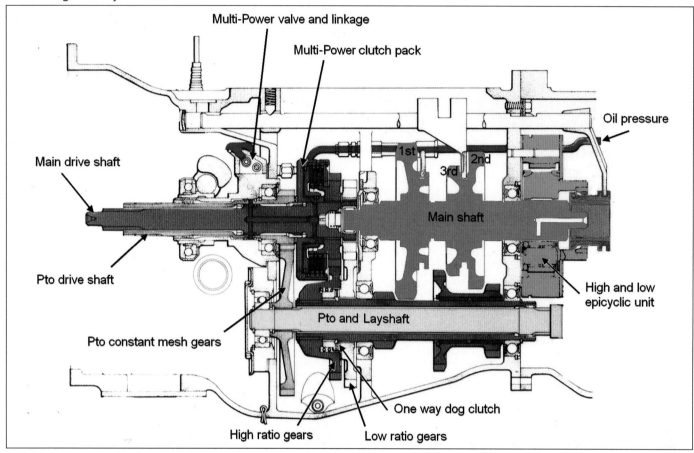

7.71. Multi-Power gearbox layout

7.72. Gearbox oil leak

the pair of gears utilised to give high and low ratios. To the rear are the conventional three-speed and high and low unit to give the mechanical six speeds.

7.72. With the tractor's engine separated from the gearbox it becomes clear that there is a major oil leak in the bell housing. The oil is light brown in colour which indicates that it is a gearbox oil leak.

7.73. One possible cause of the transmission oil leak into the bell housing and onto the clutch assembly is that the piston rings have been wearing on the input shaft and the internal scoring on the PTO shaft (the large, outer shaft). It could be that this fault led to Multi-Power oil pressure leaking past the seals.

7.74. The Multi-Power linkage from the dash-mounted lever will need to be disconnected to remove both the dash and the steering box to gain access to the gearbox internals.

7.73. Leaking input shaft

7.74. External Multi-Power linkage

7.75. Remove brake shaft

7.76. Disconnect internal oil pipe

Make a note of the orientation of the linkage. The linkage will need to be reset when refitting the dash lever.

7.75. To enable the front input shaft housing to be removed, it is necessary to withdraw both the clutch and brake linkage shafts which pass through the front bell housing. Remove the clamps, extract the woodruff keys and slide out both the shafts. This is probably the opportune time to replace the

bushes in the gearbox casing as they will be worn with age.

7.76. Before the gearbox can be separated from the rear axle casing, the internal oil feed pipe from the Multi-Power hydraulic pump, which is mounted on top of the linkage pump, needs to be disconnected from the clutch control or spool valve in the bell housing. Inspect the pipe as the rubber can perish when immersed in oil.

7.77. Selector rail layout

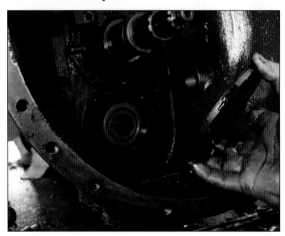

7.79. Lower shaft cover

7.78. Epicyclic unit

7.80. Input shaft

7.77. With the steering box removed, the gearbox internals are exposed. The main gear selector rails can now be withdrawn one at a time after cutting off the locking wires. The gear lever couplings and forks can be refitted as the rails are withdrawn. This enables the correct orientation and eases refitment upon reassembly. If in any doubt use masking tape secured to each rail. The three detents at the front of the gearbox lock or hold the selected gear into position; this prevents it jumping out of gear. Obviously if your gearbox does this, the detents, springs and/or the selector rails will need to be replaced. Use a small magnet to withdraw the detents from the gearbox casing.

7.78. To dismantle the gearbox, first remove the rear high/low reduction unit. Remove the two bolts at the top of the rear casing. These hold the interlock unit which will allow only one gear to be selected at a time. Slide out the high/low selector rail, turning it through 90 degrees, and unbolt the gear lever coupling on the shaft inside the gearbox. Fully withdraw the selector shaft and unbolt the high/low reduction unit keeping the parts together for inspection later.

7.79. Remove the clutch operating linkage then unbolt the left-hand side brake linkage and remove the arm and key.

Slide the shaft out from the right-hand side. Remove the lower round cover and snap ring and, using two slave set bolts (⁵⁄₁₆ x 3 in UNC), withdraw the bearing housing. Remove the thrust washer, noting that the raised edge faces toward the front of the tractor.

7.80. Remove the lower snap ring from the PTO shaft and gently tap it forwards using a soft faced copper hammer. This will allow the drive gear to drop down and enable the top input shaft housing to be withdrawn when the four bolts, Multi-Power linkage and hydraulic pipes are removed. Note the position of the washer on the rear of the input shaft as shown.

7.81. Multi-Power clutch

7.81. To disassemble the Multi-Power clutch, first remove the drive gear. Depress the clutch retainer plate in a vice and remove the snap ring with a small screwdriver. On a clean bench, lift off the parts and keep them in order. Remove the six springs, three clutch discs and three clutch plates. Inspect the plates for wear and 'blueing', caused by slipping and heat build up, and check the spring lengths.

7.82. With the rear epicyclic reduction unit remove the top shaft of the gearbox; you should be able to slide it rearwards out of the casing and then remove the top gears from the gearbox. Refit them to the shaft to keep in the correct order. Slide the inner input shaft rearwards out of the gearbox and remove the Multi-Power clutch pack.

Now the lower gears are exposed. From the lower front hole remove the snap ring on the front of the overdrive gear and move the gear assembly towards the rear of the gearbox. Then remove the unit. After the snap ring on the lower shaft is removed, the lower gears can be taken out.

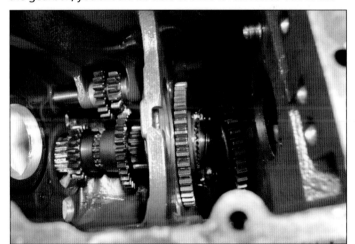

7.82. Multi-Power gear

7.83. One way clutch

7.83. This is the one-way drive dog clutch which enables the two differing ratio Multi-Power gears to be in constant engagement. When in low the drive is through this dog clutch and to the rear Multi-Power gears. When high is selected, the drive is passed to the front set of gears, but because the Multi-Power gears are in constant engagement, or mesh, in both sets the dog clutch is automatically disengaged by the higher speed of the high Multi-Power front gear. This allows a high ratio to be achieved. Although this dog clutch is in constant use, very little wear actually occurs.

7.84. To remove the piston, invert the housing and tap sharply on a wooden block or bench to shock it from the housing. Use a small pick to remove the two inner piston rings and the large outer one.

7.84. Replacing piston rings

7.85. Rebuild the Multi-Power clutch pack

7.86. Multi-Power input shaft wear

7.87. Lock tight to seal housing

7.88. Protecting input shaft seals

7.85. Reassemble the piston into the housing using three small screwdrivers to push in the large outer piston ring; the inner rings will pop into place due to the taper on the outer ring. Fit one of the new clutch plates into the housing and lubricate with clean oil. Place the six springs evenly around the housing and alternatively install the three clutch friction plates separated by the clutch plates. Refit the snap ring in the vice and twist the drive gear as you put it into the housing to align the splines.

7.86. The piston rings on the smaller input shaft should be replaced as a matter of course. On this tractor the rings are worn and showing signs of not sealing as an oil leak into the clutch bell housing is evident. If the larger outer housing is

found to have grooves internally caused by the piston rings then it must be replaced or a good second-hand one fitted.

7.87. The larger input shaft (PTO) to the left of the picture also utilises piston rings to seal the oil pressure to the Multi-Power clutch pack (approximately 20 bar or 280 psi) and they will require replacing. The two oil seals need to be replaced: the larger outer one is glued onto the end of the housing and then a press is used to fit the seal squarely onto the housing.

7.88. When assembling the input housing, use masking tape to protect the new seals from the sharp splined edges of the shafts. Do not put on too much tape as it will be difficult to remove and lubricate before assembling.

7.89. Fitting brake shaft

7.89. The gearbox can now be rebuilt using the new parts. Keeping the parts in order and marking them makes reassembly much easier. Always use new snap rings as the old ones will stretch when removed. Fit new locking wire to the selector fork bolts to prevent them unscrewing.

7.90. With the tractor gearbox rebuilt the operation of the Multi-Power can be checked. Before the rebuild you should adjust the operating lever and external linkage if necessary. This is carried out by loosening the lock nut on the top of the rod as it enters the gearbox. Flip the dash lever up to the 'high' position and push the rod down into the gearbox, the lock nut can now be retightened and the lever operation tested.

7.90. Testing after rebuild

Chapter 8 Rear Axle and PTO

This section details the strip down and repair of the rear axle casing, drive line and PTO as fitted to the MF 35 tractor. The tractor that is the subject of the step-by-step pictorial overhaul in this chapter is not fitted with the modern standard option of a differential lock because of its age (1959). The standard fitment of the very useful differential lock was not available until 1962 on the MF 35 models. Please make note of this when comparing your tractor components to the ones used in the photographs.

To gain access to the rear casing components it is easiest if the gearbox is separated at its rear end. Removing the foot plates and wings also helps make the rear components more accessible; therefore making the job easier overall. The rear hydraulic arms are first removed at the ends of the hydraulic top cover arms. Be aware that the pins may be seized in the castings and require oxy-acetylene heat to free them. The lower link arm pivot pins, on the bottom of the trumpet housings, are usually worn because of their position. These will need to be replaced once the trumpet housings are removed from the central casing.

Take extreme care when removing the axle trumpet housings because, once removed, they can make the centre casing unstable. It is advisable to use strong wooden blocks and axle stands to prevent the centre casing from falling. The hydraulic top cover can be lifted off by two people, but it is much easier and safer if a lifting crane is utilised.

Tools required for checks:

- Range of imperial spanners and ⅜ and ½ sockets
- Torque wrench
- Lifting crane and straps
- Spring balance
- Hydraulic bearing puller
- Hydraulic press
- Pillar drill
- Top cover lifting bracket
- Hammer and a small chisel
- Oil seal removing tool
- Oil seal dolly

Once this tractor was stripped down, it was obvious that it suffered from the common fault of oil leaking onto the brake shoes and back plates. The oil comes from the centre axle casing and indicates that both the trumpet housing oil seal – which is relatively easy to replace – and the outer half shaft hub oil seal is leaking. The latter part is more difficult to repair because the locking collar needs to be removed and a hydraulic press (or similar device) is required to pull the hub off the half shaft and to press the new bearing back onto the shaft.

The drum brakes can be overhauled by fitting new shoes or by re-riveting the old back plates. See Chapter 9 for more information on brakes.

To overhaul the rear axle casing follow the pictorial procedure:

8.01. Bolts to remove

8.01. The hydraulic top cover is removed to gain access to the centre casing components. Slacken off all the bolts on the outer edges in an even, diagonal pattern and remove the front right-hand rectangular cover together with the long steel pipe. Do not slacken or remove the four nuts marked in white as these hold the lift cylinder in place.

8.02. The left-hand-side PTO lever engagement cover and the right-hand-side transmission dipstick cover should be removed to assist in the dismantling of the rear axle.

8.03. The hydraulic top cover can be lifted up and away from the centre casing by using a screwdriver or chisel to wedge the spring-loaded pump actuating lever towards the rear of the tractor, away from the pump body. Using a lifting crane, carefully raise the cover clear of the casing. Place it upside down on a bench to protect the delicate linkage. Note the use of a lifting bracket fitted to the seat; this ensures that the bolts remain in position.

8.02. Remove side covers

8.03. Remove hydraulic cover

8.04. Internal parts exposed

8.05. Remove hydraulic pump

8.04. With the cover off the internal parts are exposed. If the gearbox is not being removed, then remove the torque tube split pin, slide the tube forward and pull the drive shaft out of the rear of the gearbox. Lift away the assembly.

8.05. If the gearbox is separated from the rear casing, it is easier to work on the parts. The hydraulic pump is held in position by two locating pins on either side of the casing. Remove these and lift out the pump unit.

8.06. Remove the brake drums and strip down the brakes, taking note of the spring positions beforehand. Use a piece of twine and the handle of your hammer to lift off the strong springs. (For information about overhauling the brakes see page 148.

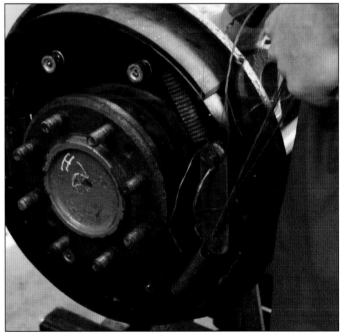

8.06. Remove brakes

8.07. Remove hubs

8.08. Remove the differential

8.09. Remove PTO hub and shaft

8.10. Remove drive gear

8.11. Remove pinion

8.07. With the brakes removed, the back plates and half shafts can be withdrawn after unbolting the hubs from the trumpet housing. Make a note of the number of shims that are fitted between the housings as they will be required when refitting the components.

8.08. To prevent damage or injury when removing or refitting the diff assembly – a heavy and awkward unit – use a long suitably sized bar to lift the diff in and out of the casing. Note: it will only come out the left-hand side.

8.09. Remove the four nuts securing the inner check chains and lift off the PTO hub cover. Pull on the PTO shaft and it should come out of the casing with the rear bearing and inner seal hub. The wear collar on the PTO shaft can be tapped off and a new one fitted. The hub seal can be lifted out with a hooked seal puller and a new seal gently tapped into position. Replace the outer 'O' ring as well.

8.10. To check the input pinion gear: first fold back the lock tabs, gently tap the locking collar anti-clockwise and slide the ground drive gear off the shaft.

8.12. Differential bearing wear

8.13. Drill collar

8.14. Press off hub

8.11. Remove the six bolts securing the pinion bearing to the axle casing and lift out. Inspect the bearings for wear and/or pitting and replace if necessary.

8.12. On inspection if the differential bearings are found to be badly pitted due to moisture and age, it is necessary to pull these off the ends of the diff with a hydraulic bearing puller and replace them with new bearings. Note: if your tractor is fitted with a differential lock, then the bearings will be different diameters.

8.13. To facilitate removal of the shrunken collar on the axle half shaft, the collar is first marked with a centre punch. Then a drill on a long extension bar is used to drill into the collar. A cut with a cold chisel into the drill hole will loosen the collar to enable it to be lifted off the shaft.

8.14. The hub now has to be pressed off the axle half shaft, supported in a suitably sized hydraulic press. If the old bearings are found to be serviceable they will require the metal swarf to be cleaned out after the drilling of the collar.

8.15. (See photo on page 142.) With the hub removed the outer seal can be extracted and the outer bearing cup tapped out. Carefully, using the old bearing, press the new cup into position and fit the new seal with a small amount of grease to lubricate it. Refit the hub onto the half shaft and grease the new bearing, using the press to push the bearing into position. Next fit the securing collar by gently heating it up to an even purple colour using oxy-acetylene gas or a propane plumber's torch. Then tap it into position. Note: do not use too much heat as this can adversely affect the outer seal.

8.15. Remove cup and seal

8.16. Remove outer seal

8.16. The outer trumpet housing seal is easily removed using a suitable length of bar. Use a socket or seal dolly to ensure the new seal is tapped into position squarely.

8.17. The differential bearing cup can also be removed with a suitable length of bar and the new one pressed into position using the old one as the guide. Note that the lower linkage arm pivot pins have been replaced as the lock nut can only be accessed once the trumpet housing is removed from the centre casing.

8.17. Remove bearing cup

8.18. Replace brake shaft bush

8.18. With the trumpet housing removed it is easier to access the brake shaft bushes located in the end of the housing. Tap them out using a small chisel and then carefully refit the new ones with a suitably sized bar.

8.19. An ideal time to replace the lower link arm pivot pins is when the trumpet housing has been removed from the centre casing. The pins are held in place by a taper pin and nut. If you only need to replace the pins, remove the left-hand trumpet housing and diff, the right-hand pin can then be removed using a socket and long extension bar.

8.20. Using the hydraulic pump locating pins as a guide, use thin (0.20 mm) paper to cut out two new gaskets.

8.21. If the pump output is below specification, there are two options. One is to replace the pump completely and two is to strip down the pump and overhaul (see Chapter 10 – Hydraulics for more details). The new pump differs slightly from the old one in that it is now fitted with a suction filter which will hopefully prolong its lifespan. It is a direct replacement.

8.22. With the PTO hub seals replaced the shaft can now be refitted to the tractor. The cover fits neatly over the hub to locate it in place.

8.23. With the pinion bearings reassembled the preload needs to be adjusted. With the diff out of the axle, lubricate the bearings and tighten the lock nut until a constant pull on the spring balance reads 8–10 kg (18–22 lb). This is the correct 'nip', or preload, required for the bearings. Bend over the locking tabs to secure the collar.

8.24. Fit new gaskets to the trumpet housings and refit the right-hand side first, tightening the bolts to 96–103 Nm (70–75 lb-ft). Position the shims between the housing and the brake back plate and carefully slide the half shaft into the hole taking great care not to damage the inner seal with the shaft. Refit the differential using the long bar as per the removal technique. Fit the left-hand trumpet housing and brake components. Tighten a few of the locating nuts to 69–76 Nm (50–55 lb-ft).

8.25. With the half shafts fitted, the end floats need to be checked; they should be

0.051–0.203 mm (0.002–0.008 in) when measured with a dial gauge. If such a gauge is not available, then the main aim is to provide a slight amount of free play to prevent the ends of the half shafts touching and welding together!

8.26. When all the components are re-assembled the centre casing can be rejoined to the gearbox. Put the PTO and gear levers into gear and align the lower shafts. Push the two casings together and, at the same time, turn the rear PTO to engage the splines. Fit the bolts and tighten to 65–73 Nm (47–53 lb-ft). Note that two of the bolts are tight in the casing holes and act as alignment studs. Slide the output shaft into the gearbox and ensure the torque tube split pin hole is facing toward the front of the tractor. Slide the tube towards the rear and fit a new split pin.

8.19. Replace lower arm pivots

8.20. Make new gasket

8.21. Old and new pump

8.22. Refit PTO cover

8.23. Preload pinion

8.24. Fit half shafts

8.25. Check end float

8.26. Refit to gearbox

Chapter 9 Brakes

The 14-in brakes fitted to the Massey Ferguson 35 tractor are of the drum brake type; they can be operated independently of each other in the field to aid turning by means of separated brake pedals. Remember that they must be locked together for safe road work. A latch is fitted to provide a parking brake to hold the pedals down when stationary. **Note: the industrial versions of the tractor may be fitted with hydraulically operated dual brakes to give more efficient braking – this version is not covered in the manual.**

🔧 Tools required for checks:

½, ¾ drive socket set

Brake retaining spring tool

Trolley jacks and axle stands

Axle wedges

Imperial and/or metric spanners

Brake cleaning fluid

Copper grease

Oil can

SYMPTOM	FAULT	REMEDY
Poor stopping – drum brakes	Contaminated linings oil, grease or water on shoes.	Remove grease/oil/water contamination; check rear axle hub seal.
	Worn linings.	Replace shoes.
	Seized linkage.	Check operation and free off with oil.
	Incorrect adjustment.	Adjust as per text.
	Glazed linings.	Rough surface of linings and re-adjust.
Tractor pulls to one side when braking	Brake balance incorrect.	Re-adjust as per text.
	Contaminated linings on one side.	Opposite side to 'pull' contaminated; clean/repair leak or replace shoes.
	Seized linkage.	Check operation and free off with oil.
	Independent pedal latch off.	Re-connect and test.
Brakes squeal	Vibration between locating pins and shoes.	Lubricate parts with copper grease.
	Dust in drums.	Remove with brake cleaner.
	Linings worn down to rivets.	Replace shoes or linings.
Brakes harsh in operation	Uneven wear on linings due to incorrect adjustment.	Reset brakes as per text.
	Seized linkage.	Check movement of all linkage and free off.
Brakes bind	Brake adjustment too tight.	Slacken off brakes and re-adjust.
	Shoes return springs weak.	Replace spring sets.
	Brake pedal(s) not returning to off position.	Check for free movement of linkage and free off.
	Handbrake seized.	Check operation and free off.
Brake judder	Loose rivets on linings.	Replace shoes/linings.
	Sticking linkage.	Check for free movement of linkage and free off.
	Rust on internal surface of drum.	Clean off with abrasive paper.
	Contaminated linings: oil, grease or water on shoes.	Remove grease/oil/water contamination.

If the drum brakes show any of the symptoms listed in the chart, then you will need to adjust them, check the linkages, replace the springs and operating linkages or replace the shoes/linings.

The layouts of the drum brakes on most tractors are very similar but you should never remove both sides at the same time. By removing only one side you can use the opposite side as a reference point; it is easy to forget where the springs are attached.

Safely jack up the rear of the tractor ensuring that you put wedges in the front axle to stop the tractor rocking. Also, place blocks at the front and rear of the front wheel to prevent the tractor rolling off the jack.

With the handbrake off, remove the rear wheels and slacken off the brakes by means of the rear-adjusting hole in the brake back plate. Remove the two drum retaining screws. The brake drums, due to rust, are usually found to be stuck solid to the axle hub. In order to free them apply heat to the area and then gently hammer and lever the brake drums until

they pop off. In some extreme cases – such as those involving yard scraper tractors – it will be necessary to break the drum into pieces to enable removal.

With the drums off, the brake shoe assemblies can be inspected and removed/cleaned.

Remember that some of the older brake linings are made from asbestos and therefore it is very important not to disturb the dust or breathe it in. Always dampen down with a brake cleaner spray or similar fluid; do not use diesel or paraffin as these will contaminate the linings. Brake linings or shoes made after 1992 (approximately) are asbestos free but it is better to be safe than sorry – you can never be absolutely sure how old the linings are!

To remove the shoes you will need to unhook the return springs from the shoes or anchor plates. The easiest and safest way is to use baler twine tied into a loop and hooked over a ball pein hammer head, this twine can then be positioned over the end of the spring and levered off safely. The reverse can be used for refitting.

Testing Brake Balance

After you have adjusted the brakes they should be checked for equal operation. With the brake pedals locked together select low second gear (if applicable) and apply the brakes gently on a straight, level surface. Any tendency to steer off course, left or right, should be counteracted by slackening off the side it is veering towards. Do not tighten up the

ineffective side as this will cause the brakes to lock on or bind in operation.

Check the brake drums for excessive heat/binding after one hour's operation.

9.01. Safely jack up rear wheels and remove the two retaining screws from the drum. Slacken off the brake adjusters and use the threaded holes in the drum to pull them off.

9.02. If the drum is stuck fast, even applied heat will not get it off. You will have to break the rusty seal in the centre of the drum by hammering!

9.01. Remove drum screws

9.02. Removing stuck drum

9.03. Cracked brake drum

9.04. Glazed linings

9.05. Oil leak on linings from axle seal

9.06. Cracked lining and rusty drum

9.07. Worn out to 3.0 mm limit

9.08. Cleaning good linings

9.03. One of the problems with hammering the drum is that cast iron is not very forgiving and will crack. Be prepared to purchase new drums.

9.04. If the brakes have been used lightly, the friction-lining surface can become glazed or shiny. But if the thickness is within the wear limit – 3 mm (⅛ in) – then clean with abrasive paper and brake cleaner before re-adjusting.

9.05. If oil is evident on the brake linings, then the axle rear end seal is leaking and must be replaced before new shoes/ linings are fitted.

9.06. Prolonged brake operation, which can be due to over application of brakes or leaving the handbrake on, will cause the linings to overheat and crack. Also, if the tractor is left standing with the handbrake on, the linings will stick to the drums and they may pull off and crack when the tractor is moved. The only option is to replace shoes or linings and clean the drums.

9.07. These linings are worn well past the 3 mm (⅛ in) limit and need to be replaced to maintain safe operation.

9.08. The brakes on this tractor are serviceable. Note that new springs and retaining clips have been fitted recently. Ensure that the adjusters and operating cams are working correctly. Clean off with brake-cleaning fluid and then lubricate with copper grease

to ensure ease of operation. Make sure not to use multi-purpose grease as this will contaminate the linings and cause the brakes to fail.

9.09. If you purchase an old stock brake lining it could be made of asbestos material. Be very careful not to cause dust when fitting; ideally you should purchase a non-asbestos type.

9.10. Complete shoes are available for most tractors but the other option is to re-line the shoes with new brake-lining material. Care must be taken to follow procedure. Bonding of the linings onto shoes will ensure added safety.

9.11. Old linings can be removed from shoes by drilling out old, bifurcated copper rivets. The shoes need to be cleaned and a centre punch tool fabricated to flatten the new rivets in place.

9.12. Apply suitable bonding glue to both the shoe and lining then fit the rivets through the shoe and lining to align holes. Working from the centre of the lining outwards fold over the bifurcated rivet sections to secure the lining; meanwhile, secure the head of the rivet using a parallel punch held in a vice.

9.13. Completed shoe with rivets recessed into lining surface. This is the wear limit of the shoe.

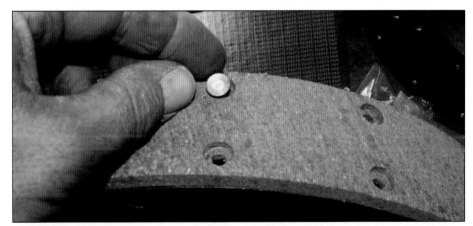

9.10. Fitting new linings

9.09. Warning asbestos lining

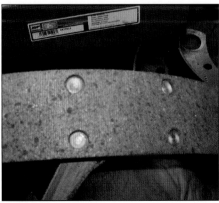

9.13. Relined shoe

9.11. Rivet tool

9.12. Setting rivets

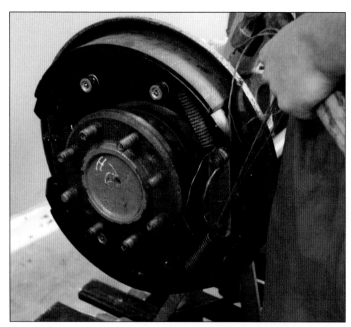

9.14. Refitting shoe

9.15. Retaining spring tool

9.16. Layout of brake parts

9.17. Fitting new drums

9.14. You should replace the brake shoes and the fitting kit (which includes the relevant springs, etc) when the linings are either contaminated with oil or worn to less than 3 mm (⅛ in) thickness. Always fit in pairs (axle sets) to ensure even braking efficiency. Lubricate pivots and joints with copper grease to ensure ease of operation.

9.15. To remove some types of shoes the retaining spring clip needs to be pushed in towards the brake back plate and turned 90 degrees. These can be difficult to refit but a tool can be purchased to make the job much easier.

9.16. Remove one side at a time to show layout of springs, etc. Note the colour of the springs and their locations. Clean all parts with brake- and clutch-cleaning fluid. The adjuster must be positioned the correct way around to line up with the hole in the back plate.

9.17. When replacing brake drums, clean off the protective shipping oil with brake cleaner to prevent contamination of linings. Ensure the retaining screws and the centre hubs are both lubricated with copper grease to prevent problems when removing drums in the future.

9.18. Slacken off the anchor pin nuts and screw steady pins into the back plate. Adjust the brake until the drum locks. Gently tap the drum all the way around and further tighten the drum then, when it will not adjust anymore, tighten up the anchor pin nuts. Screw in the steady pins until they lightly touch the brake shoes, then slacken off the brakes (with the wheel attached) until they just rub (4–5 clicks).

Road test by travelling in second gear at half engine revs then gently apply brakes; the tractor should steer in a straight line. If it pulls to one side, slacken off the side it steers to and retest.

9.18. Rear of brake

Chapter 10 Hydraulic System

The rear linkage hydraulic system fitted to the Massey Ferguson 35 is a development of the Ferguson 20 tractor system giving both draft (for soil engaged implements) and position control (for position of implements at a set height) together with the added benefits of a response control, which provides better depth and traction control. It also operates at a higher pressure of 175 bar (2,500 psi) and has an oil-flow rate of 12.72 litres/min (2.8 gpm). Later tractors from serial number 65685 onwards produced 15.14 litres/min (3.3 gpm); therefore they were capable of lifting a greater load with a quicker operation.

To gain access to the rear casing hydraulic components the gearbox is separated at its rear end. The removal of the foot plates and wings helps with accessibility, hence ease of working on the rear components. The rear hydraulic arms are first removed at the ends of the hydraulic top cover arms. Be aware that the pins may be seized in the castings and require oxy-acetylene heat to free them off. The lower link arm pivot pins on the bottom of the trumpet housings are, because of their position, usually very worn and these will be replaced once the trumpet housings are removed from the central casing.

Take care when lifting off the hydraulic cover from the centre casing, particularly if this is carried out manually, because of the weight of the unit. A lifting crane or hoist will make it easier and safer to carry out the task. The left-hand side PTO lever engagement cover and the right-hand side transmission dipstick cover should be removed to assist in the dismantling of the rear axle.

The age of the tractor and the fact that it was used as a yard scraper means the rear linkage has received a considerable amount of wear in its moving parts. When overhauling the linkage try to remove any excess play by the fitment of new replacement parts. To assess the wear, lift the lower link arms

🔧 Tools required for checks:

Range of imperial spanners and ⅜ and ½ sockets	Top yoke spanner
	Hydraulic press
Torque wrench	Top cover lifting bracket
Lifting crane and straps	Hammer and a small chisel
Spring balance	Honing tool
1.3 kg (3 lb) weight	Air/electric drill

and look for slack or play in the pivot points. Typically the link arm cross shaft bushes in the top cover will be worn and are easily replaced when the hydraulic top cover is removed.

Hydraulic Faults

If the link arms will not lift or will rise and then not lower:

- Remove the right-hand side cover and check that the linkage levers are moving the hydraulic pump spring-loaded valve, either of which could be sticking.
- Check that the lift arms can be lifted by hand. If they cannot then the cross shaft could be seized.
- The lift cylinder piston could be seized in which case the top cover will need to be removed to free off the linkage.
- If the operation seems jerky or slow the hydraulic pump could be damaged or worn and it will need to be replaced or overhauled.

If the lower link arms do not rise and lower in accordance with the operator levers, then internal wear of the linkage or parts has probably occurred and should be adjusted or replaced as the following pictures explain.

10.01. Hydraulic pump test

10.01. Since the hydraulic arms rise and lower with the movement of the operating lever, we know that oil pressure is present. By connecting an oil pressure gauge to the trailer tipping pipe outlet, we can confirm the operating pressure. The reading shows 2,000 psi which is below the recommended operating pressure of 2,500 psi, thus indicating a worn hydraulic pump, relief valve or internal leak.

10.02. Grab the two lower link arms and lift them, this will reveal any play in the pins and joints. In testing the tractor we found that our arms flopped and rattled all over the place – typical of a yard tractor. New arms and pins will definitely be needed. Note the oil leaking from the lower arm pins under

10.02. Check wear of link arms

10.03. Play in draft spring

10.04. Bolts to remove

10.05. Remove top cover

the trumpet housings; this indicates loose pins in the housing.

10.03. Hold the top draft spring attachment point and pull it in and out; there should be only a very small amount of free play. This tractor has lots and therefore the internal hydraulic linkage will need to be replaced.

10.04. The hydraulic top cover is removed to gain access to the centre casing components. Slacken off all the bolts on the outer edges in an even diagonal pattern and remove the front right-hand rectangular cover together with the long steel pipe. Do not slacken or remove the four nuts marked in white as these hold the lift cylinder in place.

10.05. The hydraulic top cover can be lifted up and away from the centre casing after using a screwdriver or chisel to wedge the spring-loaded pump actuating lever towards the rear of the tractor away from the pump body. Using a lifting crane, carefully raise the cover clear of the casing and because of the delicate linkage place it upside down on a bench. Note the use of a lifting bracket fitted to the seat retaining bolt position.

10.06. Hydraulic cover cross shaft wear

10.06. With the hydraulic top cover removed from the tractor, the play in the cross shaft is even more pronounced and a closer inspection revealed excessive wear to the bushes and shaft.

10.07. If the gearbox is separated from the rear casing it is easier to work on the parts. The hydraulic pump is held in position by two locating pins on either side of the casing. Remove these and lift out the pump unit. There was evidence of a slight noise from the hydraulic pump when it was on full load. The location pin was found to have broken off its outer bracket and was lodged inside the pump. A new or good second-hand support bracket will have to be sourced. Note that this pump has the addition of a small gear pump mounted on top of the linkage pump to supply oil to the Multi-Power hydraulic clutch.

10.07. Hydraulic pump location pin broken

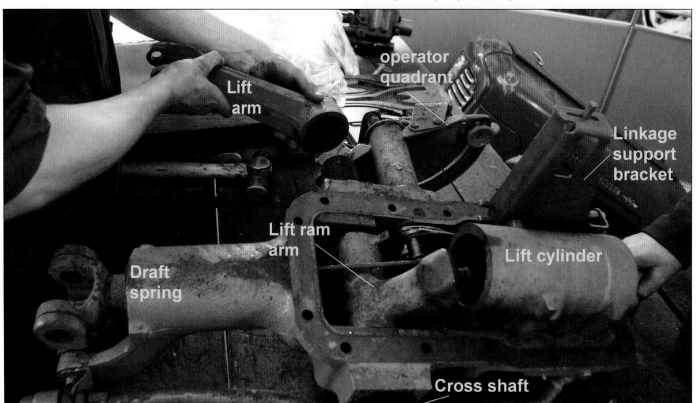

10.08. Remove arms

10.08. Mark the link arms LH and RH, bend back the lock tabs and remove the two securing bolts. Gently tap off the arms from the cross shaft. Note: sometimes heat will be required to free off the arms. Check for any play in the splines of both the arms and the cross shaft.

10.09. Remove the four nuts securing the lift cylinder to the top cover. By rotating the quadrant levers the unit can be removed with the linkage, alternatively the two bolts securing the linkage support bracket can be removed and just the lift cylinder taken off for repair. Take note of the positions or slots that the operating levers slide into.

10.09. Lift off linkage

Blanking plug

Quadrant locking screw

10.10. Remove linkage

10.11. Blow out lift piston

10.10. Remove the tapered hexagonal head screw securing the quadrant lever assembly and by rotating it through the linkage, remove it from the top cover. Remove the plug on the left-hand side of the top cover. Unscrew the grub screw from the inner casing and slide out the link shaft for the control link and roller assembly. Note that the lift cylinder 'O' ring needs to be replaced before it can be refitted.

10.12. Remove rings

10.11. Using an air line, blow out the lift cylinder piston and position a piece of wood to stop it being damaged.

10.12. Always replace the lift cylinder piston rings when dismantling the parts to this extent. Use engine piston ring expanders to ease refitment.

10.13. Hone bore

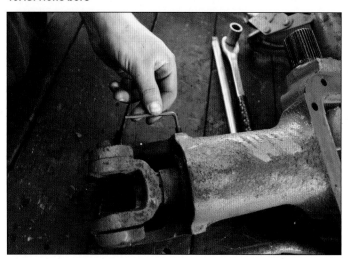

10.14. Remove grub screw

10.15. Layout of parts

10.16. Fit new cross shaft

10.17. Fit new yoke

10.13. Before refitting the lift cylinder piston, hone out the internal bore to provide a fresh surface in which the rings can bed. To do this use an engine cylinder bore honing tool.

10.14. To remove the draft control spring, first slacken the small locking grub screw, and then unscrew the retaining nut using a pegged spanner or hammer and punch. Note: the screw will normally require heating to free it off.

10.15. If you are fortunate the cross shaft will slide out of the bushes and ram arm. Normally, however, a hydraulic press is required to move the shaft out of the lift ram arm.

When refitting the parts ensure the master spline is positioned in the lift ram arm correctly and the offset middle splines are facing toward the right-hand side of the tractor. When refitting the new bushes apply copious amounts of

grease to prevent seizure. Remember to fit the 'O' rings in between the two bushes.

10.16. After fitting the lift ram arm fit the left-hand lift arm and tighten the two screws, bending over the lock tabs. Fit the right-hand arm and tighten the two screws until the arms are pinched slightly, then slacken off until the arms will move without any binding. Finally bend over the lock tabs to secure.

10.17. If fitting a new spring, the internal plunger and inner yoke will also need to be renewed. To reset the unit, remove the locking pin and screw in the yoke until the spring can be turned by hand. Refit the locking pin in the yoke. Using a hydraulic press fit the outer yoke ensuring the slots are horizontal.

10.18. Before carrying out any adjustments to the hydraulic linkage the operation levers must be in their respective sector

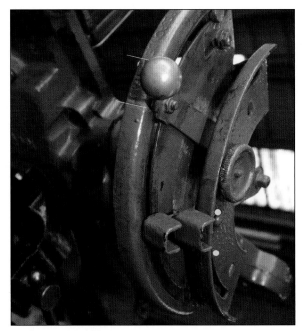

10.18. Lever positions

10.19. Adjusting draft spring

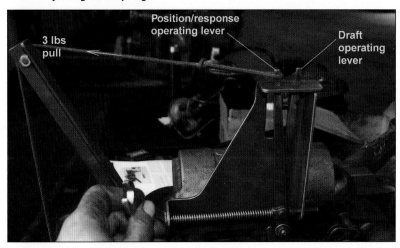

10.20. Adjust vertical levers

10.21. Adjust concentric cam

10.22. Lever position refitting

marks, i.e. the position control lever in the 'fast' position and the draft lever between the two dots.

10.19. Slacken the small grub screw and then screw in the retaining collar (with the pegged spanner or punch) until all the free play is eliminated. Be careful not to carry on tightening as the free play will increase. Tighten the locking grub screw and fit a new dirt cover boot.

10.20. Ensure the operation levers are still in the sector marks and the lift arms are in the **down** position. Slacken the concentric cam nut and slide it away from the operating arm. Using a spring balance or weight, pull 1.3 kg (3 lb-ft) towards the edge of the linkage support bracket slot and adjust the lock nut on the end of the pivot rod until the lever is just touching the end of the slot. Repeat this procedure with the other lever.

10.21. With the operation levers still within the sector marks and the lift arms in the **down** position, rotate the small concentric cam into firm contact with the cam arm. Tighten the nut ensuring the cam does not rotate. Check the operation by moving the round lever towards the 'response' position and the lever near the quadrant should move correspondingly.

10.22. Fit a new gasket to the axle casing ensuring that the hydraulic pump control valve is wedged toward the front of the tractor. Carefully lower the cover into position (guide studs will assist fitment). Refit all the bolts and tighten them evenly starting from the centre and working outwards to 62–69 Nm (45–50 lb-ft). Remove the wedge from the control valve and ensure the roller is in front of the levers. Adjust the pivot nut on the valve so that the roller is lightly touching the two levers. Finally, refit the side covers.

Chapter 11 Steering and Front Axle

The front axle assembly of the Massey Ferguson 35 tractor is a very basic mechanical steering design. The centre axle is allowed to pivot up and down and the radius rods hold the axle rigid and prevent it moving fore and aft. The ends of these rods are located in ball sockets either side of the gearbox and are part of the foot pegs.

The steering box forms the top of the gearbox casing and also houses the two gear levers. The steering wheel is connected to a shaft within the steering column and is supported at the top by a ball race; the lower end is connected via a thread to a recalculating ball nut. This in turn rotates two opposing rocker shafts onto which the drop arms and drag links are attached. As the steering wheel is turned the drop arms rotate in opposite directions thus causing the front wheels to turn at the correct angle.

Maintenance

Greasing the moving parts, adjusting the front wheel bearings and topping up the steering box oil level are simple measures to reduce wear. If play is evident when rocking the steering wheel, the box will need to be removed and stripped down for inspection. Unfortunately, the exposed nature of the steering and typical lack of maintenance has a dire consequence on the condition of the components. The

🔧 Tools required for checks:

Range of imperial spanners and ⅜ and ½ sockets	Hammer and a small diamond tip chisel
Torque wrench	Centre punch
Hydraulic press	Reaming tool
Hydraulic puller	Oxy-Acetylene welder
	Tracking gauge

drag link or steering rod ends wear out because the rubber boot perishes with age. This allows dirt and grit to wear away the internal ball and socket. Lack of grease also has the same effect. The king or stub axle pins and bushes can fill up with water and eventually seize. The wheel bearings, if not regularly adjusted, will wear rapidly and cause wheel wobble when driving along the road.

When all the components are reassembled on the steering and front axle then refitted to the engine and gearbox casing, the front wheel alignment will need to be checked and adjusted. Always torque the component nuts and bolts and check after 50 hours as they can work loose with vibration.

11.01. Remove front axle

Overhauling the steering

To overhaul the steering follow the procedure below:

11.01. Remove the four nuts and bolts of the front axle centre casting and use clamps to hold the wheels/drag links to the radius rods. The assembly can then be easily moved away from the tractor for repair.

11.02. Note: it is easy to refit the parts in the opposite positions which will result in the steering being incorrect and the wheel pointing in the wrong direction! To prevent this problem mark all similar components LH or RH (with a chisel or centre punch) when stripping.

11.03. To remove the centre axle pivot pin, first remove the shouldered retaining bolt, then using a pry bar or starting handle the pin should slide out. If it is seized in the centre axle beam then oxy-acetylene will be required to free it off.

11.02. Mark parts

11.03. Remove centre axle pivot pin

11.04. Fit new bush

11.05. New drag link ends

11.04. The centre axle pivot pin sits in a bush in the axle beam and, provided the pin has not worn through to the beam, reclamation can be made by replacing the bush with a new one using a hydraulic press. Note: two widths of bushes are used depending upon the tractor's age. Also, the hole in the centre beam must be above the centre line when refitting to the tractor.

11.05. To replace the ends, slacken off the pinch bolt, count the number of threads showing and unscrew the end. Remember one end is a left-hand thread and the other a 'normal' right-hand thread. Heat may be required to free off the seized parts. Apply copious amounts of copper grease and refit the respective ends, screwing them in until the required amounts of threads are visible. Then lightly tighten the pinch bolt and nut. Note: the cranked end joint is fitted to the steering box drop arm.

11.06. If the front axle support casting axle beam pin holes are found to be worn, sometimes a new pin will remove any wear. Alternatively the holes need to be machined and two bushes fitted or a complete new or good second-hand axle purchased.

11.07. Using a diamond chisel remove the old worn bushes carefully so as not to damage the housing. The new bushes can then be pressed into the housing.

11.06. Fit new parts

11.07. Remove king pin bushes

11.08. Ream new bushes

11.10. Rebuilt hub and arm

11.09. Thrust bearing position

11.11. Remove steering wheel

11.08. The new bushes contract when fitted and the new spindles will not fit without using reamers to carefully and accurately enlarge the bushes. (A local engineering company can perform this service.) When refitting the arms, wash out any fillings then use fresh grease to lubricate. Remember to fit the new bottom thrust bearing and top dust seal which are included in the overhaul kit.

11.09. When refitting the new lower thrust bearing, ensure it is fitted with the word 'TOP' facing upward. This orientation allows the bearing to support the load of the front of the tractor correctly. Note: the felt dust seal is shown in its working position at the top of the spindle.

11.10. Because of the wear and corrosion within the wheel hub a new one is required. When reassembling the hub, pack the space between bearings with a handful of multi-purpose grease and grease around the rear bearing before fitting the seal. Refit the hub into the spindle and fill the outer bearing with grease. Finally, fit the washer and castle nut. Tighten up the nut until there is no free play and then slacken it off until

just a very small amount is felt. Fit a new split pin. It may be necessary to slacken or tighten the nut slightly to align the hole for the split pin, but make sure the bearings are not too tight and that the wheel can rotate freely.

11.11. The steering wheel domed nut usually seizes in place and will require a long bar to slacken it. Obviously it is easier to do this with the steering box fitted to the tractor!

11.12. Carefully tap the centre boss of the steering wheel with a hammer to release it from the column. If it will not move do not hit it too hard as the plastic on the wheel will break off necessitating the replacement of the wheel. Use a small puller on the centre hub to pull it off. Once removed the dash and battery tray can be stripped from the steering box.

11.12. Strip down dash

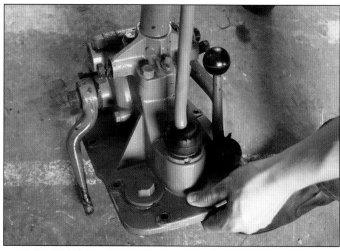

11.13. Position of drop arms

11.14. Press off arms

11.15. Side cover removed

11.16. Remove pin

11.17. Lift off steering arm

11.13. Slacken and remove the drop arm nuts. Before removing them note their relevant positions and mark the casing and the arm to ease refitment.

11.14. Use a puller to remove the drop arms from the shafts.

11.15. Remove the bolts and gently tap off the side cover, drain out the semi-fluid oil. Inspect the bushes that support the drop arm shafts for wear and if necessary remove and fit new

bushes and ream to the correct size.

11.16. Bend back the lock tabs and unbolt the ball peg. When removing the ball peg note the number of shims fitted between the peg and the lower gear.

11.17. Remove the four bolts securing the outer steering column to the box and lift away with the inner shaft and reciprocating ball nut.

11.18. Layout of steering column

11.19. Fit steering column

11.18. Straighten the tab washer and remove the top bearing lock nut, adjustable ball race nut and race. Remove the 12 steel balls and the lower race, ring and cup oil seal. If the lower nut is removed ensure you collect the 28 steel balls. Replace any worn parts and inspect the steering column shaft ball race thread for wear, especially in the middle section where most of the steering operation occurs. When refitting, grease the races and balls and tighten the nut to eliminate any free play but not too tight to pinch it. Fit the lock nut and finally bend over the lock tab.

11.19. Fit the new oil lip seals to the steering box housings. Using electrical tape wrap the splines to protect the seals. Fit the inner ball peg to the lower drop arm shaft and slide it into place. Lower the steering column (with the chamfered edge facing forwards) ensuring that the ball nut on the column is at the top of the thread. Fit the outer ball peg with the old shims. Check that it is free to rotate without any play, then add or remove shims as required. Remember to bend over the locking tabs.

11.20. Fit the upper drop arm shaft and mesh the gears as shown. Apply gasket sealer to a new housing gasket and protect the lip seal using electrical tape as before. Fit the side cover and refit the drop arms as they were marked before disassembly.

11.21. The names of the steering component parts, which vary depending upon manufacturers' descriptions, can cause problems when ordering new parts.

11.22. With the dash panel refitted and the throttle lever refitted, the wiring can be reconnected. A new woodruff key is fitted to the column shaft and a new chrome washer and domed nut are also fitted and tightened.

11.20. Position of gears on refitment

11.23. The final task is to check and adjust the front wheel alignment to ensure even tyre wear and correct steering. The front wheels should be parallel or point towards each other slightly (toe-in). Use a gauge or steel tape to measure the front and rear distances at the centre of the wheel rims. The difference should be between 0 and 3 mm (0 and ⅛ in). To adjust the alignment, slacken the drag link's pinch bolts and turn the rods clockwise or anti-clockwise to increase or decrease the toe-in. Roll the tractor forward and check. Then tighten the pinch bolts if correct.

11.21. Position of arms

11.22. Refitted

11.23. Tracking checked

Chapter 12 Electrics

The 12-volt electrical system fitted to the Massey Ferguson 35 tractor is a simple dynamo charging layout and can be a pre-engaged starter motor fitted with a safety switch on the high/low gear lever for the 3- and 4-cylinder diesel engines, or on the petrol/TVO engine an inertia engaged starter motor and separate solenoid. The only other option available is a lighting kit which includes side lights mounted on the wings and round front headlamps on top or sides of the bonnet. This is operated via a switch fitted to the dash.

Battery Repair Tips

When the cold weather sets in you may find that the lead acid battery in your vehicle has lost its 'get up and go' – the operator can be similarly affected! Low temperatures combined with engine-oil drag can reduce the power that the battery supplies to the starter motor. Modern farm equipment is utilising more electronics in the operation of the engine, transmissions and hydraulics; this increase in electronics combined with the extensive use of powerful work lights means that the battery is in constant use and needs to be in tip-top condition.

Unfortunately, if the battery terminal connections, starter motor terminals or the earth point have a high resistance because of corrosion or loose connections, then no matter how good or powerful the vehicle's battery is, the resistance will prevent full power going to the starter motor. This means that the engine will not turn over at a sufficient speed to enable it to fire and start up.

🔧 Tools required for checks:

¼ Whitworth spanner

Range of metric spanners and socket sets

Flat blade screwdrivers

Protective gloves

Electrical terminal cleaner or petroleum jelly

To ensure your vehicle starts first time, the battery needs to be fully charged. There are two things you can do to achieve this. First, ensure the warning light extinguishes when the engine starts and second, check that the generator drive belt is tight, in good condition and free from oil or grease.

Vibration is one of the major enemies of the lead acid battery. It causes the internal plates to fall apart, shorting out the internal parts and reducing battery life. To avoid this, ensure the retaining strap or clamp is fitted to the battery casing.

Batteries that are old or are not able to hold their charge will not turn over the engine fast enough. The power that is available in your battery can be measured by using a simple LED unit or a professional heavy load tester. If necessary replace with a new battery of equivalent size or power. See www.vapormatic.com/assets/documents/vapormatic_batteries.pdf for applications. Some batteries will have a small 'state of charge' light that informs the operator of the current condition of the battery and can help determine whether the battery requires replacing.

Disposal of a Lead Acid Battery

Once a battery reaches the end of its lifecycle and needs replacing, it is removed from the vehicle and becomes quarantined for disposal. Lead acid scrap batteries are considered hazardous waste. In order to properly dispose of them you must follow a legally specified procedure. Take them to a local recycling centre. The battery supplier has a legal obligation to collect the old battery and can issue an environmental certificate as evidence of disposal.

12.01. The sulphuric gas, moisture and the lead battery terminal will cause corrosion or 'fur'. This will lead to a high resistance and poor starter motor performance. Wash off the corrosion

12.01. Corroded battery terminal

12.02. Poor starter connections

12.03. Bad earth bolt

using either bicarbonate of soda or washing powder mixed with hot water. Clean completely with emery paper and smear both terminals with petroleum jelly or battery electrical grease to prevent it happening again.

12.02. On agricultural vehicles the starter motor is exposed meaning that corrosion can quickly occur. First, disconnect the battery earth lead to prevent sparks and fires. Then remove the connections and clean with emery paper. Finish by coating in a protective grease to prevent recurrence.

12.03. The earth strap from the negative battery terminal is usually attached to the metal chassis of the vehicle. Ensure yours does not look like this one! Poor earth connection will slow the starter motor speed and the voltage loss will also affect the electrics on the vehicle.

12.04. The heavy-duty load tester will test the power available from the vehicle's battery and will show whether the battery is failing when under load. It can also test the charging output.

12.04. Test battery power

Inertia Starter Test and Repair

If your tractor is difficult to start because of slow cranking speed, it could possibly be the connections or the battery condition or age. Once you have tested and determined that it is the starter, you have a few choices for how to deal with the situation.

1. Fit a second-hand unit of unknown condition or reliability;

2. Fit a new unit (but this will not be of the same design/layout as the original);

3. Recondition your old unit and maintain the unchanged appearance of your vehicle.

🔧 Tools required for checks:

Range of imperial spanners and ⅜ and ½ sockets

Screwdrivers

Multi-meter

Electrical cleaner

Lathe

Soldering iron

Battery tester

To test the inertia starter system

It is very important to remember that the starter motor is only designed to be operated for a maximum of 30 seconds, after which it should be allowed to rest and cool down to prevent internal damage. If the vehicle will not start when the ignition switch (or lever) is operated, then you should refer to the faults and remedies listed in the tables.

FAULT	POSSIBLE CAUSE
Starter does not operate or clicking noise is heard.	• Battery
	• Connections
	• Solenoid is faulty
	• Ignition switch
	• Internal fault
Starter turns slowly.	• Battery
	• Connections
	• Contamination
	• Internal fault
Starter motor is noisy in operation.	• Mounting bolts are loose
	• Spring is broken
	• Ring gear is damaged
	• Starter pinion is damaged
Starter turns but engine does not rotate.	• Ring gear or starter pinion is damaged
	• Starter drive clutch
	• Internal wiring
	• Solenoid is faulty
	• Operating level linkage is worn

FAULT	INTERNAL FAULT	REMEDY
Starter motor does not operate when battery cable is directly connected with terminal stud of connector (contact) blade.	a – Brushes sticking	a – Clean brushes and guides of brush holders
	b – Brushes worn	b – Replace brushes
	c – Weak spring tension; brushes do not make contact	c – Replace springs
	d – Commutator dirty	d – Clean commutator
	e – Commutator rough, pitted, or burned	e – Recondition starter motor
	f – Armature or field coils defective	f – Overhaul starter motor
Sluggish or slow action of the starter motor.	a – Battery run down	a – Charge battery
	b – Insufficient current flow due to loose or corroded connections	b – Clean battery terminals and cable clamps, tighten connections
	c – Brushes sticking	c – Clean brushes and guides of brush holders
	d – Brushes worn	d – Replace brushes
	e – Commutator dirty	e – Clean commutator
	f – Commutator rough, pitted, or burned	f – Recondition starter motor
	g – Armature or field coils defective	g – Overhaul starter motor

12.05. Battery top-up and test

12.06. Earth voltage drop

12.07. Fitting reconditioned starter

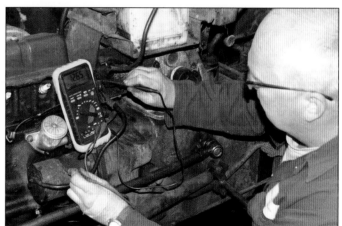

12.07a. Testing Solenoid

12.05. Before carrying out any tests on the starter, the condition of the battery must be tested using a battery hydrometer. Ensure the battery is fully charged before continuing. Connect a multi-meter to the battery terminals and set to DC voltage. Turn on any electrical loads (e.g. lights, wipers or crank engine) for 1–2 minutes and check that battery voltage maintains between 12 and 12.9 volts, thus indicating a good voltage.

12.06. Connect the multi-meter between the battery earth terminal and the starter earth or body. When the starter is operated the reading should be nearly zero (0.004 volts in picture). If the reading is high check all connections, including the battery, and the earth straps.

12.07. Due to the way that engines are balanced, the starter usually stops in one of two positions. This unfortunately wears the starter flywheel ring gear teeth, which should be inspected through the starter hole in the bell housing prior to fitting a new starter as the ring gear will damage the new pinion teeth on the new starter.

12.07a. Pull out the stop lever, or disconnect the fuel cut off, so that the engine cannot start. The voltmeter should read about 9.0 to 10.0 volts.

A low reading indicates excessive current flow in the circuit due to a fault. The result is that the starter will probably turn slowly.

12.08. Remove brushes

12.09. Insulation damaged

12.10. Field insulation perished

12.11. Worn brushes

12.12. Bodged brushes

12.13. New brushes

12.14. Concaved commutator

12.15. Skimming commutator

12.16. Clean commutator

12.17. Electrical cleaner

12.08. To dismantle the starter motor, first remove the dust steel band. Then, using a 'G' shaped hook, remove the brushes from their holders.

12.09. One of the faults found with this starter was that the insulation had broken down around the main live terminal connection. This could possibly have led to an electrical short or burnt out starter.

12.10. The field winding insulation has perished. This could be due to old age or it may have occurred because of the live terminal damage caused by an internal short in the starter that overheated the windings.

12.11. If you find that the starter motor turns slowly but the other parts of the circuit are still functioning correctly, then the problem could be worn brushes in the motor. When they reduce in length from 8 to 10 mm ($\frac{5}{16}$ to $\frac{3}{16}$ in) – depending upon motor size – the brushes should be replaced in sets. Note: the tool made from $\frac{1}{16}$ welding wire that is used to hook the brushes back against the spring for ease of replacement.

12.12. At some point in the life of this starter motor the brushes have been 'repaired'. Instead of soldering the new brushes to the

terminals, the wires were twisted together and because of the high current flow this caused internal damage.

12.13. This is what the new brushes and connections should look like after a professional overhaul.

12.14. This is typical uneven wear of the armature commutator. Over time the brushes have worn the copper surface. Before the new brushes are fitted, they must contact the whole surface of the commutator; therefore, it needs to be machined to remove the uneven surface.

12.15. The commutator of the old starter armature can be restored to a clean parallel shaft if it is fit to a lathe and machined.

12.16. As the brushes wear, the spring cannot put enough pressure upon the commutator. This then burns due to arcing and leads to poor starter motor speed and torque. The commutator can sometimes be repaired by cleaning with fine glass paper.

12.17. To remove any traces of grease, oil or metal dust on the parts of the starter motor an electrical or brake and clutch cleaner should be used.

12.18. Checking front bearing

12.19. Pinion wear

Worn brushes and poor connections

Concaved surface of commutator

Worn front bearing

Breakdown of field winding insulation, damage insulation to feed connector

Damaged teeth on gear

12.20. Starter faults

12.18. To dismantle the starter motor, first mark the housing to aid alignment upon refitting and then remove the two long screws. Using the 'G' shaped tool remove the brushes and lift away the end plate. Pull the field windings from the armature and then the front bearing can be checked as shown.

12.19. A new pinion and recoil spring has been fitted to the original reconditioned starter to replace the one with worn and damaged teeth.

12.20 & 12.20a. When the starter motor was disassembled these are the faults that were uncovered. In order to bring the machine condition back to new, the faulty starter components were either repaired or replaced.

12.20a. Old and reconditioned

Pre-engaged Starter System Test and Repair

🔧 Tools required for checks:

Range of imperial spanners and ⅜ and ½ sockets	Small screwdrivers
	Multi-meter

When restoring the electrical system of the Massey Ferguson 35 tractor always ensure all of the old components are working satisfactorily if they are going to be refitted. Before carrying out repairs on any part of the electrical system, you should always disconnect the battery terminals to prevent risk of damage to the components or to the tractor. Touching the live wires onto the metal chassis will cause sparks, or worse a fire hazard, as the wiring will overheat. Make sure to disconnect the earth wire first when disconnecting the battery. If you intend to replace the battery, be aware of the original size of the old one as the space under the bonnet is tight. If the new battery is too tall or too long the battery terminals will touch the metal bonnet and this could short out the battery with disastrous consequences.

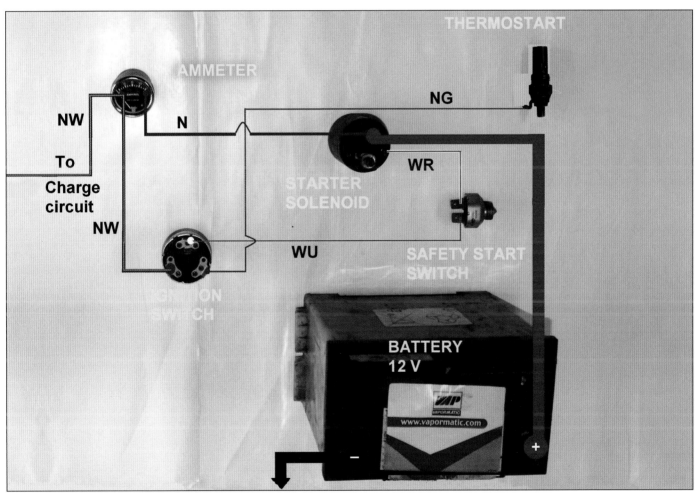

12.21. Wiring diagram

To fully test the starter operating system, an ammeter would be ideal, but it is possible to fault find adequately with just a multi-meter.

12.21. This is the wiring for the starter circuit of the Massey Ferguson 35X 3-cylinder tractor. Note the safety start switch, which is positioned on the high/low gear lever to prevent the tractor starting in gear and moving forward, possibly causing damage. The small white and red coloured wire from the safety switch feeds the solenoid windings and operates the starter motor.

Colour wiring diagram for the Massey Ferguson 35X tractor:

CABLE COLOUR CODES			
B	BLACK	P	PURPLE
U	BLUE	R	RED
N	BROWN	W	WHITE
G	GREEN	Y	YELLOW

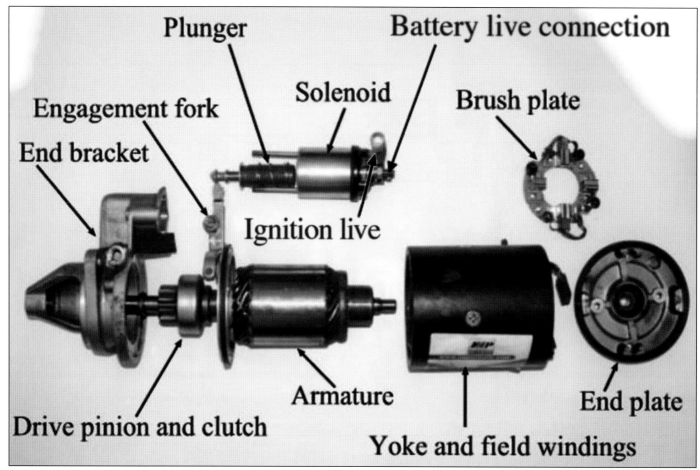

Plunger

Engagement fork

Solenoid

Battery live connection

Brush plate

End bracket

Ignition live

Armature

End plate

Drive pinion and clutch

Yoke and field windings

12.22. Exploded view of pre-engaged starter system

12.22. When the vehicle operator turns the starter key against the internal spring the starter will become operational. Voltage from the ignition switch is supplied to the small solenoid terminal connection and the plunger is then pulled back by the electro-magnet.

The engagement fork pushes the pinion into the mesh with the flywheel ring gear. At the same time, the contacts at the rear of the solenoid are bridged and allow full battery current to flow to the starter field and armature windings (via the brushes); this delivers the full torque which turns the engine. In the event that the operator does not release the starter key, a one-way drive clutch is fitted to the pinion gear to prevent the engine turning the starter when it fires.

Once the engine is running, the starter key springs back to the run position and the feed to the solenoid is disconnected. The plunger spring pulls the fork out of engagement with the flywheel ring gear and the brake at the rear of the starter slows the armature to a rest position.

12.23. If the tractor is in gear when the engine is cranked, then it can be prevented from moving with a safety isolator switch that is fitted to the top of the gearbox casing. This switch is operated by the high/low gear lever. A multi-meter set to the continuity setting can be used to test its operation.

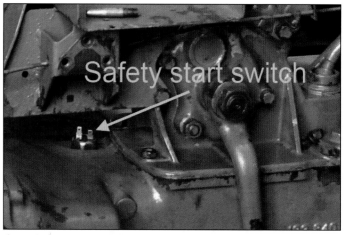

Safety start switch

12.23. Safety start switch

12.24. This clutch allows the starter to drive the engine but will freewheel if the engine fires and tries to turn the starter too fast in the opposite direction. It should be free to turn in one direction, but should lock up and drive in the opposite direction when tested.

12.25. In the rear of the end plate a centrifugal brake slows the starter motor down quickly once the operator releases the starter key. This allows the pinion to stop and then mesh again quickly if the operator turns the starter key again.

12.24. Drive clutch

12.25. Brake in end plate

12.26. Brushes and field magnets

12.28. Wear of commutator

12.26. If the starter motor turns slowly and the other parts of the circuit are ok then the problem could possibly be worn brushes in the motor. When they have reduced in length to between 8 and 10 mm (⁵⁄₁₆ and ⁷⁄₁₆ in), depending upon motor size, the brushes should be replaced in complete sets.

Note the 'G' shaped tool made from ¹⁄₁₆ welding wire which is used to hook the brushes back against the spring for ease of replacement.

12.28. As the brushes wear, the spring cannot put enough pressure on the commutator. This then burns due to arcing and leads to poor starter motor speed and poor torque. The commutator can sometimes be repaired by cleaning it with fine glass paper; do not use emery paper as this could contaminate the copper and lead to poor contact of the brushes. Finish by cleaning off the commutator with brake cleaning fluid.

12.29. Due to the way that engines are balanced, the starter usually stops in one of two positions. This unfortunately wears the starter flywheel ring gear teeth, which should be inspected through the starter hole in the bell housing prior to fitting a new starter as the ring gear will damage the new pinion teeth on the new starter.

12.29. Starter ring gear

12.30. Pinion teeth damage

12.30. Mechanical damage to the starter drive gear teeth is due to the starter turning when meshing with the flywheel ring gear. In this case you will probably need to replace the flywheel ring gear as well as the starter motor. It is possible to cause physical damage by not allowing the starter to come to rest before re-engaging it. Continuous engagement of the starter will also cause damage.

Testing the Starter Motor

It must be remembered that the starter motor is only designed to be operated for a maximum of 30 seconds, after which it should be allowed to rest and cool down to prevent internal damage. If the vehicle will not start when the ignition switch is operated, check the table for some possible faults and causes.

FAULT	POSSIBLE CAUSE
Starter does not operate or a clicking noise is heard.	• Battery • Connections • Ignition switch
Starter turns slowly.	• Battery • Connections • Contamination
Starter motor is noisy in operation.	• Mounting bolts are loose • Locating dowel is not fitted • Ring gear is damaged • Starter pinion is damaged
Starter turns but engine does not rotate.	• Ring gear or starter pinion is damaged • Starter drive clutch • Internal wiring • Solenoid is faulty • Operating lever linkage is worn

12.31. Check battery condition

12.31. First disconnect the earth terminal and then the live terminal. Note: on a dynamo charging system the earth could be the positive or negative terminal!

Check battery condition using a hydrometer; the reading should be in between the white and green sections of the float. If it is in the red section that means that the battery needs recharging from a mains charger. Make sure that the battery terminals are clean and tight. Any green 'fur' that builds up on the terminals can be washed away with hot water and washing powder.

12.32. Test 1: battery voltage

12.32. Connect a multi-meter to the battery terminals and set to DC voltage. Turn on any electrical loads (e.g. lights or wipers) for 1–2 minutes and check that the battery voltage maintains between 12 and 12.9 volts, thus indicating a satisfactory voltage level.

12.33. Pull out the stop lever, or disconnect the fuel cut off, so that the engine will not start. Then operate the starter; the multi-meter should read approximately 9.0 to 10.0 volts. A low reading indicates excessive current flow in the circuit due to a fault. The starter will probably turn slowly.

12.33. Test 2: cranking voltage

12.34. Test 3: terminal volt under load

12.35. Test 4: volt drop on insulated line

12.36. Test 5: volt drop across solenoid

12.34. Connect the voltmeter between the starter motor input terminal – the one that disappears into the motor casing – and a good earth terminal on the body or battery. Crank the engine again with the fuel stop out. The reading should be no more than 0.5 volts lower than in the previous test. A large difference in the two readings indicates a high resistance, which means poor/loose, damaged connections or wires.

12.35. Connect the multi-meter between the motor terminal and the battery live terminal. When the ignition switch is operated a battery voltage should register (as shown in the picture). When the switch is off the reading should be practically zero. A high reading would indicate poor connections or an internal fault in the starter.

12.36. Connect the multi-meter across the two solenoid terminal studs. When the switch is operated the battery voltage should be shown (as picture demonstrates). When the ignition is off, a reading of approximately zero should be found. If not, the solenoid or connections are at fault.

12.37. Connect the multi-meter between the battery earth terminal and the starter earth or body. When the starter is operated the reading should be nearly zero (0.004 volts in picture). If the reading is high check all connections, including battery and earth straps.

12.37. Test 6: volt drop on earth line

3-Cylinder Electrics

In this section we are looking at the wiring and the dynamo charging system of the Massey Ferguson 35X 3-cylinder tractor. This is the same for all variants of MF 35 tractors.

It is important to note that if you are fitting a new dynamo, the unit needs to be 'polarised'. This involves telling the dynamo which terminal on the battery is connected to the live wire. Normally the live wire is connected to the negative terminal of the battery and the earth wire is connected to the positive terminal. Using a piece of wire, touch one end to the live battery terminal and touch the other end to the 'F' terminal on the dynamo: a small blue spark will confirm contact.

If you intend to replace the battery be aware of the original size of the old one as the space under the bonnet is tight and if the new battery is too tall or too long the battery terminals will touch the metal bonnet. This could short out the battery with disastrous consequences.

When changing the electrical connections to the new wiring loom, ensure a good low resistance connection by always 'tinning' the bare wire first. This means using heat from a

Tools required for checks:

Range of imperial spanners and ⅜ and ½ sockets

Small screwdrivers

Multi-meter

Electrical connectors

Heat shrink protective cover

Wire strippers

Side cutters

Electrical connector crimpers

Soldering iron and wire

soldering iron and applying an electrical solder to the wire. Next fit the relevant electrical connector and use a good quality ratchet crimper to give a tight secure joint. The new loom can be connected to the electrical components using the end connectors as a guide. Ensure it is routed away from the exhaust manifold and that cable ties are used to secure it in place to prevent chaffing on moving linkages.

Inspect the dynamo drive belt for cracks or oil contamination and replace if necessary. Repair any oil leaks before fitting a new belt. Usually poor charging and overheating indicate a problem with the belt drive.

12.38. Poor wiring

12.38. In the case of this tractor, forty years of wear combined with contamination by fuel leaks and ageing of the plastic covering of the copper wire on the tractor's electrics has resulted in a greater chance of the occurrence of fire or poor starting. Broken or loose wires will damage the components of the charging system, leading to increased cost when carrying out repairs.

12.39. To preserve your sanity, always label the old wiring loom as you remove the connections from the various

12.39. Label old wiring

components on the tractor electrical system. The labels can then be transferred to the new loom or used as a reference when connecting it.

12.40. Make sure to first disconnect the earth terminal to the starter and then the live terminal. Note that on a dynamo charging system the earth could be the positive or negative terminal!

12.41. Use a hydrometer to check the condition of the battery. The reading should be in between the white and green sections of

12.40. Disconnect battery

12.41. Check battery

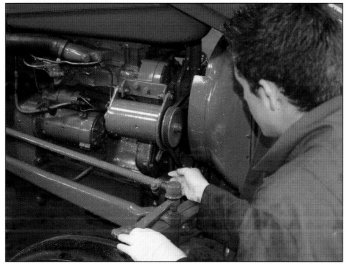

12.42. Belt tension

12.43. Quick charging test

the float. If it is in the red section, that means that the battery needs recharging from a mains charger. Make sure that the battery terminals are clean and tight. Any green 'fur' that builds up on the terminals can be washed away with hot water and washing powder.

12.42. Inspect the belt tension and adjust it if necessary by turning the dynamo on its brackets. Care should be taken not to over tension the belt; it must not be as tight as an alternator belt drive. The tension midway between the crank and dynamo pulley should be 19 mm (¾ in).

12.43. Using the multi-meter set to DC voltage, you can perform a quick test of charging voltage with the engine running at half throttle. In this case the charging system is faulty. The correct charging volts should be between 13.5 and 14.5 and this system is showing less.

12.44. Visually check the connections. If they appear dirty or have corrosion on them use electrical spray to chemically clean them. Repair any loose or damaged connectors.

12.44. Check dynamo wires

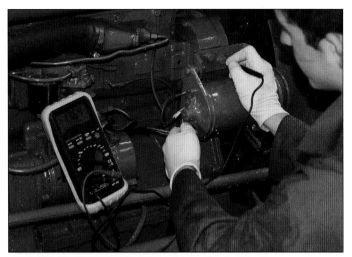

12.45. Test dynamo output

12.46. Quick dynamo test

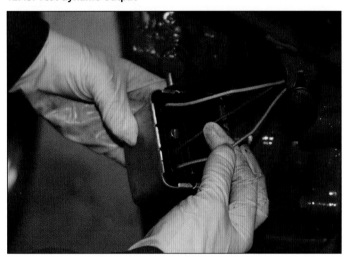

12.47. Check control box wires

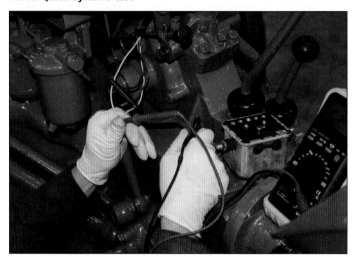

12.48. Control box D and F test

12.45. To test the dynamo output remove the two wires from the rear of the unit and, using a link wire made up with one large and one small terminal end, join the spade terminals together. Connect a multi-meter to one of the wires and start the engine at idle speed. Slowly raise the engine speed and note the reading, it should easily reach at least 16–20 volts to show the dynamo is operating correctly. If not, an inspection or the replacement of the dynamo will be necessary.

12.46. After overhauling the dynamo or fitting a second-hand unit, a quick test of the vehicle can be carried out. Clamp the dynamo in a vice and connect the jump leads to a battery. Connect one clamp to the body of the dynamo and then place the other clamp across the two terminals on the rear of the dynamo. This should make the unit turn in a similar way to an electric motor, thus confirming that it is working.

12.47. Remove the control box from underneath the dash and check the electrical connections. Ensure they are clean and tight.

12.48. Remove the F and D wires from the control box, hold them together and connect the multi-meter. Repeat the wiring test as per the dynamo test (12.45). If the reading is low, or there are no results, one or both of the wires must have a break in it. Repair the wires and repeat the test.

12.49. Replace the D and F wires into the control box and connect the multi-meter to the D output terminal and earth terminal. Start the engine and note the maximum output voltage obtained on the meter display. It should be between 13 and 13.5 volts, showing that the control box is working correctly.

12.50. The dynamo on this tractor stopped working because the tractor was stationary for a long period of time and the armature (copper part) had become dirty. Cleaning and checking over the part should get the tractor functioning again. To disassemble the dynamo, mark the housings and remove the rear end plate.

12.51. Clean off armature contacts and components with electrical cleaner. Scrub with emery paper until parts are bright and shiny.

12.52. The end plate holds the contact brushes which must be at least 8 mm (⁵⁄₁₆ in) in length. Note that the springs are holding the brushes back to allow the end plate to be refitted easily. Make sure the marks on the body – made before disassembly – are realigned. Carry out a quick test on the dynamo while it is off the tractor before refitting it to the engine.

12.49. Test 3 control box output

12.50. Mark housing

12.51. Clean off parts

12.52. End plate with brushes

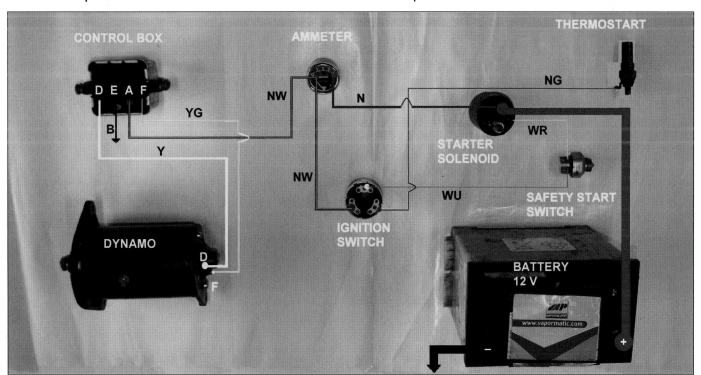

12.53. Wiring diagram MF 35X 3-cylinder diesel

12.53. (See photo on page 177.) When the ignition is off, the ammeter should show 'no charge' because it is earthed out through the dynamo. When the engine is started, the dynamo starts to generate current and therefore voltage. When this figure reaches approximately 13 volts, the control box – which controls voltage to the battery – allows this higher voltage to pass through to the battery to charge it. The ammeter will move to the + (positive charge) at the right of the gauge. If the engine speed drops to idle, then the control box will disconnect the dynamo from the battery to prevent the dynamo from discharging through it.

The control box can also vary the output of the dynamo via the 'F' field terminal, which regulates the amount of electricity flowing to the battery and prevents overcharging. This limits the voltage but is dependent on the condition of the battery – i.e. flat, half or fully charged – and the type of loads being used, i.e. lights or operation of the starter motor.

See page 169 for the colour wiring diagram for the Massey Ferguson 35X tractor starter circuit.

12.54. With the old loom removed from the tractor, unravel the new one and compare the electrical end connections. Since there are manufacturing variations of the electrical components fitted to the tractor you will inevitably find that some connections will need to be changed.

12.55. The dash can now be rebuilt using the new gauges and wiring. Note: it is a matter of choice whether you replace the tractor meter with a new one or use the old to keep originality and the correct hours of work displayed! Unfortunately, the glass had broken several years ago, making the dial unreadable on this MF 35 X meter.

The completed dash can now be fitted to the tractor and lowered onto the steering column. Connect the throttle lever and linkage at the same time. Next feed the wiring loom through its correct path on the chassis.

12.54. Comparing old with new

12.55. Rewiring dash

4-Cylinder Electrics

When overhauling a tractor's electrical system always ensure all of the old components are working satisfactorily if they are going to be refitted. Always disconnect the battery terminals to prevent risk of damage to the components or the tractor before carrying out repairs on any part of the electrical system. Touching the live wires onto the metal chassis will cause sparks or worse a fire hazard as this will cause the wiring to overheat. Always disconnect the battery earth wire first.

If you are repairing the charging system please refer to how to check and repair the dynamo system. See page 175–7. Note, if you are fitting a new dynamo, the unit needs to be 'polarised'. This involves telling the dynamo which terminal on the battery is connected to the live wire; normally with a dynamo charging system this is the negative terminal of the battery and the earth wire is connected to the positive terminal. Using a piece of wire touch one end on the LIVE battery terminal and with the other end touch the 'F' terminal on the dynamo (a small blue spark will confirm contact).

If you suspect the starter operation is poor see starter motor section for how to check and repair the system. See page

Tools required for checks:

Range of imperial spanners and ⅜ and ½ sockets	Wire strippers
	Multi-meter
Small screwdrivers	Side cutters
Electrical connectors	Electrical connector crimpers
Heat shrink protective cover	Soldering iron and wire

172. If you intend to replace the battery be aware of the original size of the old one as the space under the bonnet is tight and if the new battery is too tall or too long the battery terminals will touch the metal bonnet with disastrous consequences.

When changing the electrical connections to the new wiring loom, always 'tin' the bare wire first to ensure a good low resistance connection. See page 181. This means using heat from a soldering iron and applying electrical solder to the wire. Then fit the relevant electrical connector and use a good quality ratchet crimper to give a tight secure joint.

12.56. Disconnect battery

12.56. Always disconnect the earth terminal to the starter first and then the live terminal. On a dynamo charging system the earth could be the positive or negative terminal.

12.57. Label old wiring

12.57. To preserve your sanity, always label the old wiring loom as you remove the connections from the various components on the tractor electrical system. The labels can then be transferred from the old loom or they can be used as a reference when connecting the new loom.

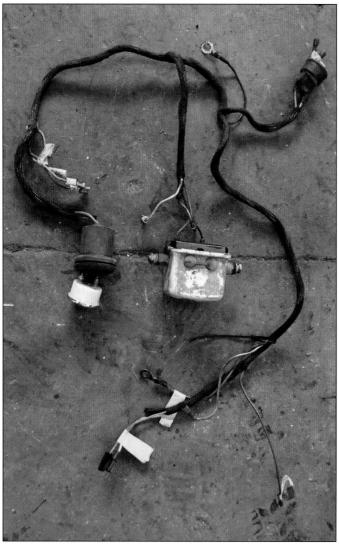

12.58. Old loom

12.59. Comparing old with new

12.60. Rewiring dash

12.58. Once disconnected, the old loom can be removed from the tractor; this one is probably not the original loom as the wire colours tend to bleach with time because of dirt, diesel oil and sunlight. As you remove the loom note the route that the various wires follow through the tractor chassis: you will have to replicate this when fitting the new loom.

12.59. With the old loom removed from the tractor, unravel the new one and compare the electrical connections. You will inevitably find that some will need to be changed because of the different types of manufacturing variations of the electrical components fitted to the tractor.

12.60. The dash can now be rebuilt using the new gauges and wiring. It is your choice whether or not to replace the tractor meter with a new one or keep the old one for originality.

12.61. The completed dash can now be fitted to the tractor and lowered onto the steering column. Connect the throttle lever and linkage at the same time. Next feed the wiring loom through its correct path on the chassis.

12.61. Dash fitted

12.62. Connecting components

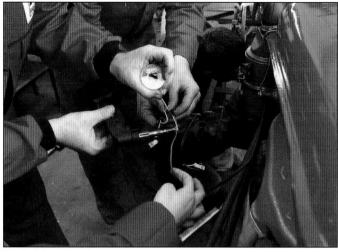

12.63. Extending loom

12.62. Using the end connectors as a guide, the new loom can now be connected to the electrical components. Ensure it is routed away from the exhaust manifold and that cable ties are used to secure it in place to prevent chafing.

12.63. If the wiring loom needs to be altered, or in this case extended, ensure a soldered joint is used to give a good low resistance connection. Tin the ends of both wires and fit a heat shrink sleeve. Then melt the solder to join the two ends.

12.64. With the soldered joint made, a heat shrink sleeve is fed over the joint, with at least 25 mm (1 in) overlap, and heat is applied to form a watertight joint. Various sleeve sizes are available depending upon the diameter of the wire.

12.65. The colour wiring diagram for the Massey Ferguson 35 4-cylinder diesel engine. (See page 184 for the table.)

12.64. Using heat shrink cover

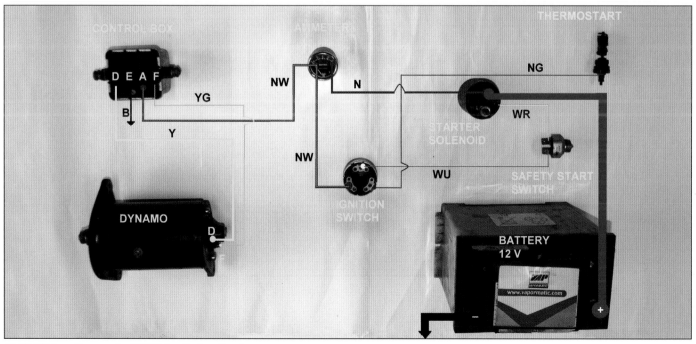

12.65. Wiring diagram for MF 35 4-cylinder diesel

Petrol/TVO Electrics

Remember to follow the same procedure and guidelines specified for the 3-cylinder and 4-cylinder Massey Ferguson tractor electrics overhaul.

To assess the running of the engine remove the spark plugs and check their condition against the plug colour chart. See original Champion spark plug faults below.

Normal

Combustion deposits are slight and not heavy enough to cause any detrimental effect on engine performance. Note the brown to grayish tan colour, and minimal amount of electrode erosion which clearly indicates the plug is in the correct heat range and has been operating in a 'healthy' engine.

Mechanical Damage

May be caused by a foreign object that has accidentally entered the combustion chamber. When this condition is discovered, check the other cylinders to prevent recurrence, since it is possible for a small object to 'travel' from one cylinder to another where a large degree of valve overlap exists. This condition may also be due to improper reach spark plugs that permit the piston to touch or collide with the firing end.

Oil Fouled

Too much oil is entering the combustion chamber. This is often caused by piston rings or cylinder walls that are badly worn. Oil may also be pulled into the chamber because of excessive clearance in the valve stem guides. If the PCV valve is plugged or inoperative it can cause a build-up of crankcase pressure which can force oil and oil vapours past the rings and valve guides into the combustion chamber.

Overheated

A clean, white insulator firing tip and/or excessive electrode erosion indicates this spark plug condition. This is often caused by over advanced ignition, timing, poor engine cooling system efficiency (scale, stoppages, low level), a very lean air/fuel mixture, or a leaking intake manifold. When these conditions prevail, even a plug of the correct heat range will overheat.

Insulator Glazing

Glazing appears as a yellowish, varnish-like colour. This condition indicates that spark plug temperatures have risen suddenly during a hard, fast acceleration period. As a result, normal combustion deposits do not have an opportunity to 'fluff-off' as they normally do. Instead, they melt to form a conductive coating and misfire will occur.

Pre-Ignition

Usually one or a combination of several engine operating conditions are the prime causes of pre-ignition. It may originate from glowing combustion chamber deposits, hot spots in the combustion chamber due to poor control of engine heat, cross-firing (electrical induction between spark plug wires), or the plug heat range is too high for the engine or its operating conditions.

Gap Bridging

Rarely occurs in automotive engines, however, this condition is caused by similar conditions that produce splash fouling. Combustion deposits thrown loose may lodge between the electrodes, causing a dead short and misfire. Fluffy materials that accumulate on the side electrode may melt to bridge the gap when the engine is suddenly put under heavy load.

Splash Fouled

Appears as 'spotted' deposits on the firing tip of the insulator and often occurs after a long delayed tune-up. By-products of combustion may loosen suddenly when normal combustion temperatures are restored. During hard acceleration these materials shed from the piston crown or valve heads, and are thrown against the hot insulator surface.

Detonation

This form of abnormal combustion has fractured the insulator core nose of the plug. The explosion that occurs in this situation applies extreme pressures on internal engine components. Prime causes include ignition time advanced too far, lean air/fuel mixtures, and insufficient octane rating of the gasoline.

Ash Fouled

A build-up of combustion deposits stemming primarily from the burning of oil and/or fuel additives during normal combustion... normally non-conductive. When heavier deposits are allowed to accumulate over a longer milage period, they can 'mask' the spark resulting in a plug misfire condition.

Carbon Fouled

Soft, black, sooty deposits easily identify this plug condition. This is most often caused by an over-rich, air/fuel mixture. Check for a sticking choke, clogged air cleaner, or a carburetor problem – float level high, defective needle or seat, etc. This may also be attributed to weak ignition voltage, an inoperative preheating system (carburettor intake air), or extremely low cylinder compression.

Worn

This plug has served its useful life and should be replaced. The voltage required to fire the plug has approximately doubled and will continue to increase with additional miles of travel. Even higher voltage requirements, as much as 100% above normal, may occur when the engine is quickly accelerated. Poor engine performance and a loss in fuel economy are traits of a worn spark.

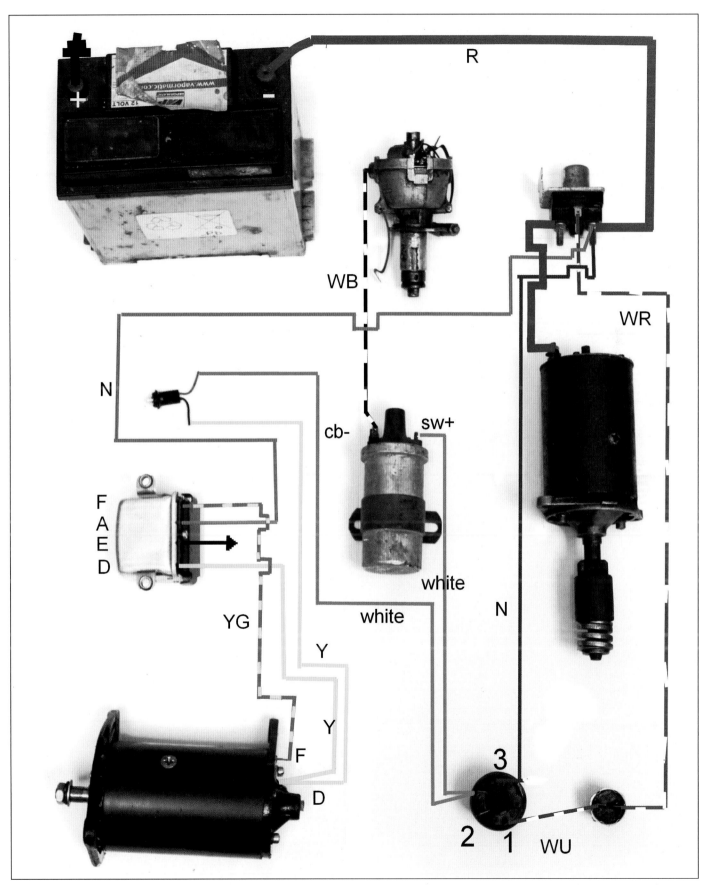

R

WB

WR

N

cb-   sw+

F
A
E
D

white

N

YG

white

Y

N

Y

F

3

D

2   1   WU

12.66. MF 35 petrol/TVO wiring diagram

12.66a. Poor leads

12.66b. Faulty plug lead

12.67. Distributor cap

To check the ignition timing see how to set up the distributor in Chapter 4 – Engines, on page 65.

12.66. (See photo on page 183.) This is the wiring for the starter circuit of the Massey Ferguson 35 petrol/TVO engine tractor. Note the safety start switch, which is positioned on the high/low gear lever. This prevents the tractor starting when in gear and moving forward, possibly causing injury or damage.

Colour wiring diagram for the MF 35 petrol/TVO tractor:

CABLE COLOUR CODES			
B	BLACK	R	RED
U	BLUE	S	SLATE
N	BROWN	W	WHITE
G	GREEN	Y	YELLOW
P	PURPLE		

12.68. Rotor arm

12.66a. A misfire, poor starting or engine performance can be attributed to a break down of the HT (High Tension) spark plug leads.

12.66b. The HT spark plug leads can be checked for resistance using an Ohm meter; they should measure in the range of 5 to 10 kΩ. When it comes to spark plugs, replacement rather than repair is usually the best option. Over time the insulation breaks down and the high voltage (up to 25,000 volts) escapes leading to a loss of spark at the plug.

12.67. If the engine is having similar performance issues to the spark plugs (mentioned on page 182), then the distributor cap could be allowing the voltage to track or escape. Clean the terminals inside the cap when inspecting and ensure the centre carbon pin is moving.

12.68. This rotor arm distributes the spark to the relevant HT lead inside the distributor cap as the engine revolves. It has an insulated brass contact on the top and this can cause misfire, etc. If in doubt, replace it.

12.69. Remove low tension nut

12.70. Remove the cb point's adjustment screw

12.71. Lift out base plate

12.72. Layout of parts

The round cylinder in the background is the condenser; this prevents the spark arcing across the contact breaker (cb) points as they are opened by the cam in the centre of the distributor. If they are found to be burnt when you are removing or inspecting the cb point then the condenser should be replaced. Note: they can also cause a misfire and this would be evident because a yellow spark would appear at the plug when tested instead of a bright blue one.

12.69. To remove the cb points, first remove the low tension wire nut, insulation washer and second nut. This will allow the spring to slide out of the post.

12.70. Remove the cb point's adjustment screw and the screw securing the base plate.

12.71. Lift out the base plate, noting the position of the insulation washer. Clean any oil or dirt from the internals of the distributor.

12.72. Check the new parts against the old to ensure they match and refit the parts in the correct order. Leave the adjustment screw loose.

12.73. Reset gap

12.74. Carbon fouled plugs

12.75. Gap

12.76. Gap tool

12.73. To set the gap of the cb points rotate the engine until one of the cam lobes is forcing the brown cb arm out. Using a 0.356 to 0.406 mm (0.014 to 0.015 in) feeler gauge, adjust the gap and then tighten the base screw and check the gap.

12.74. The dry black coating on these spark plugs is typical of an engine that has been running for short periods or one that has had the choke pulled out for too long. The solution is either a good clean with a soft brass wire brush or to replace them. Either way, set the gap from 0.03 to 0.032 in (0.76 to 0.81 mm).

12.75. Use a feeler gauge set to 0.03 to 0.032 in (0.76 to 0.81 mm).

12.76. If it is too loose, tap the bent earth electrode on a hard surface to close the gap. However, to open the gap if it is too tight, DO NOT lever between the centre electrode and the bent electrode, instead use a gap adjusting tool, as shown, as a lever.

Chapter 13 Bodywork

In this chapter a combination of informative text and clear pictorial procedures will enable you to understand the steps that are necessary to restore the bodywork of a Massey Ferguson 35 tractor. When restoring the bodywork and chassis we may be reusing the original parts because it adds to the originality of the tractor.

This chapter will also provide tips on how to paint new panels, not only to prevent corrosion of the parts but to prolong the life of the metal as well as make the tractor look good.

Bonnet Repair

Tools required for checks:

Oxy-acetylene welder

Bronze and mild steel filler rods

Protective welding goggles

Fire extinguisher

Small 4-inch angle grinder

Cutting and grinding discs

Electrical or air sander

Body panel tools

Wet and dry sandpaper (various grades)

Painting equipment – spray or roller

Body filler

The major dilemma when performing any restoration on the bodywork of a classic tractor is whether to purchase new parts or take the time to repair the tinwork in order to keep the tractor as near to its original form as possible. Obviously, the cost of new purchases could be prohibitive or else the part may no longer be available. New parts will never be exactly the same as the original parts and sometimes they can even be a slightly different pattern, which affects originality. For example, some of the new pattern parts do not have the starting handle hole supplied in the front lower panel. If you have patience and time, then the skills can be practised to achieve a high quality of finish – plus you will experience the satisfaction of doing it yourself.

The condition of the tractor bonnet was such that welding needed to be carried out. Oxy-acetylene welding equipment gives you more flexibility in both gas and bronze welding processes. It will also be needed to apply heat to manipulate the tinwork back to the original shape. The equipment for this process can be hired from local companies or if you plan to use it more frequently, which you will when you have discovered how useful it is, it can be purchased from various fuel gas suppliers. Training in its use should be gained from a knowledgeable friend or local college to ensure safe operation. The high temperature of the flame (3,200 °Celsius) is a dangerous fire hazard and must be treated with respect. Flammable material should never be positioned near the flame.

The other pieces of special equipment used in the restoration of bodywork are panel-beating hammers and dollies; both have curved faces and shapes for manipulating the metal back into shape. Tractors have thicker panels than those used in the bodywork of cars and special equipment is used with the assistance of heat to shape those thicker panels. The secret is to manipulate the metal in the opposite way to the way that it was forced out of shape, i.e. to its original position. After bringing the panels back to original shape, body filler – or leading for a truly rust preventative finish – is used to smooth the surface imperfections to produce a flat and even surface for painting.

One important consideration when repairing the bonnet is to maintain its shape with the instrument cowl and the front mounting holes. Both of these must be carefully kept in line and can also act as a guide when reshaping.

13.01. Typical yard scraper

13.02. Close inspection

13.03. Close inspection side view

13.04. Badge area damage

13.05. Lower panel corrosion

13.01. (See photo on page 187.) The frame on the front of the axle has protected the bonnet from physical damage, but unfortunately the layers of FYM have a very corrosive affect on the metal work.

13.02. On closer inspection, the side and front panels have been bent and severe corrosion has occurred.

13.03. Although bent, the side panels and bonnet area have not suffered any serious corrosion and can therefore be cleaned, straightened and resprayed.

13.04. This close-up shows the damage to the badge area. Also there is a twist to the top end of the grill recess as it slopes toward the lower right-hand side of the picture.

13.05. After cleaning, the front lower panel was found to have more severe corrosion than first thought – usually the case! This means that the corroded front lower panel will need cutting out and a new piece will have to be welded in.

Apply heat to this area to re-form shape

13.06. To re-form the side and front panels, heat needs to be applied to the thick metal areas where it has been bent (see the highlighted areas in the picture). The hammers and dollies can then be used to gently reshape back to original position.

13.07. The side and front panel left-hand edge has now been bent back to original shape. Now the lower edge needs to be removed with a cutting disc. Then it should be cleaned of rust ready for a new plate to be inserted.

13.06. Side and front panel dent

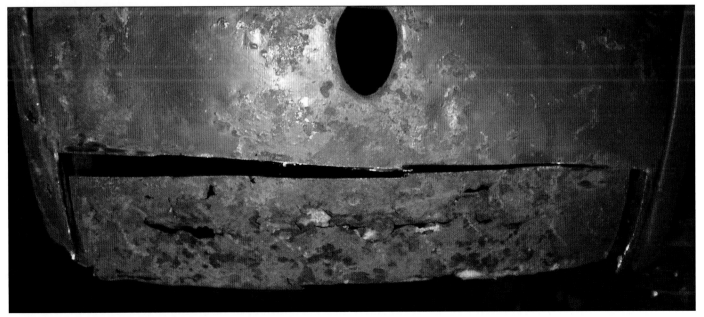

13.07. Side panel straightened and front has rust cut out.

Hand sanding block

Orbital Sander

Wet and dry sanding paper grades: 60, 180, 320, 1000.

Coarse sander

Body re-forming hammers and dollies

13.08. Panel and bodywork tools

13.08. These are the range of tools and equipment, which assist the repairing of the panels together with the oxy-acetylene welder and body filler.

13.09. After removing the corroded section a new plate is cut to size and gas welded into position. Tack welds are used to hold the plate in the correct position before carrying out a continuous weld. Note the use of bronze welding to join side and front panels as per original manufacture.

13.10. The lower edge of the front panel (where it joins the reinforcing rear member) also required repair and plating. Bronze welding is particularly useful for thin areas of metal, due to the lower heat applied, and forms a good anti-corrosion base.

13.11. After all the welding has been completed the areas are sanded back to remove high spots ready for the application of body filler.

13.12. If panel beating and welding has been carried out successfully, only a small amount of filler will be required. Use different grades of wet and dry sandpaper (starting with 60 or 180 grade then onto 320) to produce a smooth, even surface ready for painting with primer.

13.09. New front plate welded in

13.10. Lower edge plated

13.11. Ready for filler

13.12. Filled and ready for sanding back

13.13. Top coat side view

13.13. After applying a coat of primer and sanding back with 320 grade wet and dry sandpaper, the top coat of machine enamel is applied and allowed to dry to a tacky finish. Apply another coat around three to four times to give depth and finish to bonnet. Sometimes it is necessary to flatten the panels back with 1,000 grade wet and dry sandpaper with soapy water; this will help to remove slight imperfections.

13.14. Most of the dents in the bonnet panels have been removed but the small ones have been left to retain the character of the original tinwork.

13.14. Front view top coat

13.15. Finished ready for shows

13.15. Once the chassis and wings have been finished and reassembled the tractor is ready for shows.

13.16. Close up of finished tractor

13.16. This is the result of all the hard work: a good-as-new bonnet which is still the original. Note: badges and transfers have yet to be added.

Paintwork

It is important to apply a protective coating to the tractor to prevent corrosion. Before we can apply the top coat of shiny paint, we must ensure all traces of oil, grease, loose paint and rust have been removed to allow for the adhesion of the paint. The easiest and most effective way to achieve this on major components is to shot blast the parts. There are local companies that will produce a spotlessly even, clean and slightly rough surface onto which primer paint will stick brilliantly without the hard work normally required when using an angle grinder, sanding discs, paint stripper, wire brushes and scrapers. The shot blasting will also very quickly uncover thin rusted areas of the panels and what initially

13.17. MF 35 before restoration

🔧 Tools required for checks:

Range of imperial spanners and ⅜ and ½ sockets

Flat and Philips blade screwdrivers

Hammer and small chisel

Sanding disc

Wet and dry sandpaper

Spray gun, regulator and air compressor

Shot blaster

appears to be slight surface corrosion on the bonnet can turn into large rust holes. So beware what lies beneath when you pick up the parts from the shot blaster!

One word of caution: if grit that is too coarse or, worse, steel shot is used, this will make the shot blaster's job easier but will dent the soft metal panels. These panels will then require additional filling and priming to produce an even, un-pitted finish. In other words, more work for you.

To achieve a smooth surface finish to panels such as wings, bonnet and cowling, it is important that you apply a layer of primer to the surface and then flatten it back with medium fine wet and dry paper (360 grade). This will also remove the slightly rough textured surface left after shot blasting the panels.

The wheels are removed and the chassis placed on axle stands, which are high enough to allow for painting underneath. Primer is applied to all surfaces. A minimum of 4–5 litres is required to give a suitable thickness, with a ratio of 10% thinners to allow paint to flow from the paint gun. This is then allowed to dry, the speed of which will be dependent upon the air temperature. It is advisable to try to paint with a minimum temperature of 12°–15 °Celsius. Painting the chassis is easier than the flat panels; however, it is important not to over apply paint as this will lead to the overloading of the surface of the panel causing runs, which give a poor finish. It is easier for a novice sprayer to apply less paint and simply increase the number of coats. Allow the paint to achieve a dry, tacky finish between coats to gain depth and shine.

The panels – such as bonnet, dash, grill and wings – require a greater level of skill/attention to prevent runs caused by over-application of paint. If runs do occur then try brushing them out when paint is wet or allow them to dry and flatten with 320 grade wet and dry sandpaper. Practice makes perfect when spraying, so experiment on flat scrap surfaces first.

Allow the whole top coat of paint to dry for at least two days, or longer if possible, to prevent damage to the paint when fitting the parts back onto the tractor. Finally, the transfers can be applied.

13.18. Side panel condition

13.19. Remove old cab wings

13.20. Hand paint chassis

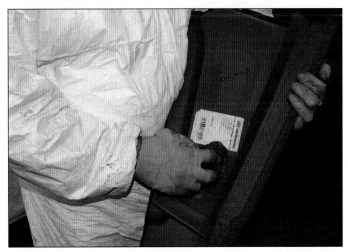

13.21. Remove labels

13.17. Before restoration the tractor appeared to be in reasonable condition, but on closer inspection it was found to have problems with poor engine starting, worn brakes and rear hydraulics. The tin work consisted of the remnants of a tractor cab and a well-used tractor bonnet.

13.18. The bonnet side panels show typical corrosion around the locating bolt holes and also 'crash' damage. The lower front panel has a temporary repair, which covers the rust on the bottom edge. The top of the bonnet is in reasonable condition, but the front nose has been pushed in; therefore, a complete new bonnet assembly will be fitted.

13.19. As new wings are to be fitted to the tractor, the old cab wings are removed together with the cab frame. Because of the specific age of the tractor, late 1963, it is conceivable that it could have been fitted with either shell or full rear wings. Shell wings will be fitted this time.

13.20. Once the chassis has been steam cleaned to remove all traces of loose rust, oil, grease and paint, it is possible, with enough paint brushes, to get a reasonable finish to the chassis components.

13.21. As the bonnet assembly is unwrapped, the panels reveal sticky identification labels; these are removed using white spirit or paint thinners. Ensure all the glue is removed from the panel.

13.22. Transit scratches

13.23. Flatten back and degrease

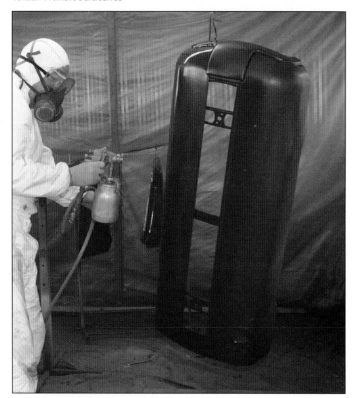

13.24. Prime bonnet

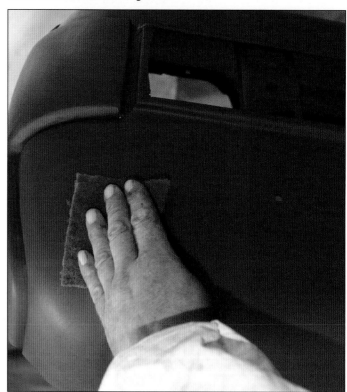

13.25. Flatten back primer

13.22. As the panels are unwrapped there will always be evidence of light paint damage due to delivery handling, these will need to be smoothed flat to prevent them being highlighted by the top paint coat.

13.23. The brown primer is only sufficient to protect the panels in storage and delivery. This primer should be flattened back using 360 wet and dry sandpaper, providing a key (or roughened surface), for the new primer to be applied. It should also be degreased using white spirit or paint thinners.

13.24. With the correct protective equipment worn and using a home-made spray booth, the bonnet is suspended to permit ease of painting both the inner and outer surfaces.

13.25. Let the paint dry overnight or for two to three hours, depending upon the outside temperature; ideally the temperature should be above 12°–15 °Celsius. Once the paint is dry, the primer is rubbed down again with 360 grade wet and dry sandpaper or sanding pad to produce a smooth surface ready for the top coat.

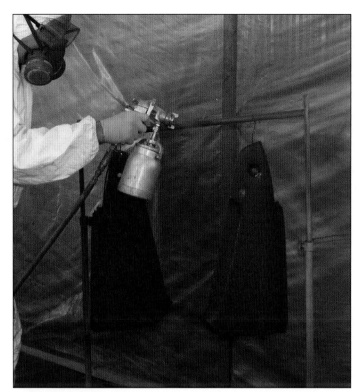

13.26. Prime side panels

13.28. Apply top coat

13.27. Wings and tanks

13.29. Rear wheels

13.26. Make sure to clean, sand and degrease the side and front panels before applying brown primer.

13.27. The use of work benches and purpose-built stands enable the parts which are to be painted to be held in such a position to make the painting process and coverage easier.

13.28. Painting the chassis is easier than the flat panels. When painting the wings and bonnet it is important not to over-apply paint as this will lead to more runs than the Olympic games (!) and give a poor finish. See section introduction on page 194 for more tips on painting.

13.29. The rear wheels are easier to paint and handle without the centres attached to the rims. Apply the same method used on the new bonnet: flatten back the shipping primer and degrease before painting with primer and top coat.

13.30. Shot blast chassis

13.31. Painting chassis

13.32. Rebuilding tractor

13.33. Finished product

13.30. The most effective way to remove old paint and rust is to use a shot-blasting unit. The parts that need to be sealed are blocked off or protected from the shot using strong tape. After several hours of blasting, the bare metal chassis will be revealed; it needs to be primed immediately or it will start to rust.

13.31. The chassis is covered with two to three coats of grey primer and to ensure complete coverage a layer of beige primer is added last. Then two to three layers of Stoneleigh grey top coat are applied. For the final coat 70% yacht varnish is added to produce the shiny finish. The steering drag link and radius arms can be unbolted to permit full paint cover.

13.32. With the chassis and bodywork painted, the tractor can finally be re-assembled. Note: some of the parts have been painted individually to allow non-painted or zinc-coated nuts and bolts to be used as per the original factory assembly.

13.33. The final result.

Fitting a New Bonnet

If you want to restore your tractor as close as possible to its original state, then always try to restore the original panels. Items such as the grill and chrome parts can easily be substituted with new parts that will have little effect on originality. Unfortunately bigger parts, such as a new replacement bonnet, will never have the same fit and contours as the original design due to manufacturing variations.

If the bonnet is in good condition but the other panels are corroded or damaged, then fitting new sides or lower panels could be a viable compromise. The only major problem that could require a new top bonnet assembly is if the front nose is pushed inwards – a common and unfortunate issue for yard scraper tractors with no brakes! A pushed-in front nose is extremely difficult to reshape because of the thickness of the metal and the internal formers.

As this tractor is under complete restoration and the original bonnet is beyond economic repair, all the body panels will be replaced. Remember to allow the paint to cure and harden for at least two days, or longer if possible, especially if the outside temperature is below 20 °Celsius. This will help to prevent damage to the paint when assembling the parts and fitting the bonnet onto the tractor.

🔧 Tools required for checks:

Range of imperial spanners and ¼, ⅜ and ½ sockets

Flat and Philips blade screwdrivers

To ensure full coverage of Massey Ferguson red, which will protect the bare metal, the bonnet assembly panels are sprayed individually. The parts are then assembled together to produce the completed tractor bonnet. When assembling the new bonnet parts, do not fully tighten the retaining fixings until you are happy with the way that the panels align with each other. Use the front grill to give the correct positioning of the bonnet, sides and lower panel. Then fit the assembled bonnet to the tractor to assist in the final position with the dash cowl. After this, the retaining fixings can be fully secured.

The transfer positions can be determined by consulting old brochures, magazines or unmolested/original tractors. Using pictures taken at shows can also help aid reference at a later date. In order to preserve the originality and to allow for your tractor to be used as a reference point for restoration you should not restore a tractor that is in good used condition. It also demonstrates the fit and location of the tractor panel gaps together with the correct position and type of transfers on such items as the oil and air filters.

Follow the pictures to rebuild the Massey Ferguson 35 bonnet and fit to the tractor.

13.33. Unmolested tractor

13.34. Offering up side panel

13.33. Unmolested tractors, such as this one seen at the 2010 Newark tractor show, enable us to ensure that our restoration is an accurate replication of the panel gaps, alignment and transfer placement. It is unnecessary to restore this well cared for example owned by just one family.

13.34. With the bonnet supported on a suitably sized work bench, the side panels can be trial fitted to the front. Note the diagrams showing the layout of the parts that will be fitted to the completed bonnet.

13.35. Lining up side panel

13.37. Fit upright rubber

13.36. Top wing nuts

13.35. Fit the three nuts and bolts to the left and right side panels. With a little bit of jiggling the gap and the line-up of the panels with the bonnet can be arranged.

13.36. The lower front panel can now be fitted and the side bolts and wing nuts installed. Once the alignment of the edges and 'square-ness' is ensured, the fittings can be tightened lightly. Make sure to note the lower rubber strip attached to the lower panel.

13.37. The rubber strips on the side and lower panels prevent the bonnet rubbing on the side of the radiator and causing damage to it. Fit the special clips evenly to the edges and then slide in the rubber trim, fat edge first.

13.38. The final check to confirm that the side, front and bonnet are aligned correctly is to fit the front grill. The gap all around the grill should be even and should fit flush with the front edge of the red panels.

13.39. The top inspection hood is held in place by two catches that are locked into position by 'S' shaped spring wires. Take care to fit the springs in the correct orientation, as shown, to enable the levers to twist and pull down the hood securely.

13.40. The original bonnet hood catch levers are fixed to the hood by means of Dzus clips. The name is pronounced Zooss and is a proprietary name for a type of quarter-turn fastener. These were held in place originally by a special aluminium grommet which is crimped into place, thus holding the lever in position. Unfortunately, it is difficult to do this without the special tools; therefore, an alternative is to file or saw a groove in the lever that is wide enough to accept an external circlip to secure it in place.

13.41. After the groove has been made in the lever, a fibre washer is fitted to lift the lever away from the hood panel to prevent scratching. Then the circlip is attached.

13.42. Place the bonnet upside down onto a soft, large piece of cloth and then assemble the hood and hinges with the domed chrome bolts, nuts and thick washers as shown.

13.43. There is sufficient movement of the hood bolts to allow movement to ensure it is sitting square on the bonnet opening. Once satisfied with the fit, the bolts can be fully tightened.

13.38. Trial fit grill

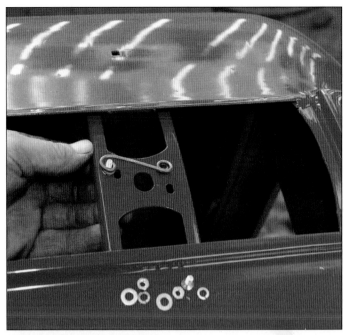

13.39. Fit bonnet catch springs

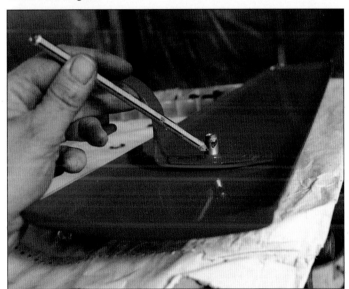

13.40. Bonnet catch groove

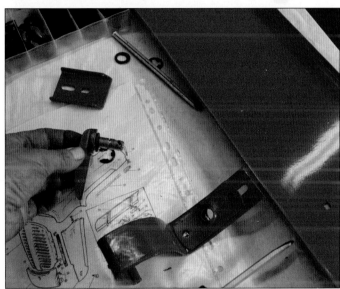

13.41. Bonnet clip arrangement

13.42. Fit dome bolts

13.43. Lining up flap

13.44. Check fit

13.45. Carefully fit bonnet

13.46. Adjust bonnet to fit dash panel

13.47. Line up air cleaner with hole

13.44. After fitting the inspection hood, the two levers must be checked for correct location and when turned they should pull down the flap onto the bonnet. If this is not possible, the spring clip needs to be slacked off and then realigned.

13.45. Carefully fit the bonnet at an angle onto the front axle casing and lower the rear end down onto the dash. Lift up the front edge of the bonnet and secure lightly with the special shouldered bolts making sure that they locate into the holes in the left- and right-hand side panels.

13.46. In theory, the bonnet should line up with the dash panel evenly. If there is a small discrepancy it can be corrected by moving the dash on the retaining bolts. This is where cheap, low quality bonnets fail because the positioning and alignment of the front holes on the side panels magnifies the level of errors.

13.47. The air cleaner pre-cleaner pipe should line up with the hole in the bonnet. If it is found that the pipe is in the wrong position, the air cleaner clamp can be slackened and the pipe aligned correctly.

13.48. The front Massey Ferguson badge is located on the front of the bonnet and holes are pre-drilled to give the correct position.

The pins pass through the bonnet and can be securely held by the spring clips as shown.

13.49. Original sales brochures, pictures or un-restored tractors can be used to mark the correct position of the transfers on the bonnet.

13.50. Clean the bonnet with degreasing fluid to ensure the transfer adhesive will adhere to the bonnet. Apply warm water with washing-up liquid on the bonnet and then peel the backing strip from the transfer and apply it to the panel.

This method will allow you to move the transfer around to the correct position before using a clean cloth or de-icer rubber squeegee to remove the air to allow the adhesive to stick the transfer to the bonnet.

13.51. The last job is to fit the bonnet catch rod and wing nuts to either side of the bonnet. They prevent the bonnet flipping forward if the vehicle has to stop suddenly.

13.52. These are the nuts and bolts, rubber trim and clips which are supplied with the Vapormatic bonnet assembly. They replicate the original fittings.

13.48. Clips to hold front badge

13.49. Fit transfers

13.50. Slide transfer on

13.51. Fit bonnet tie clamps

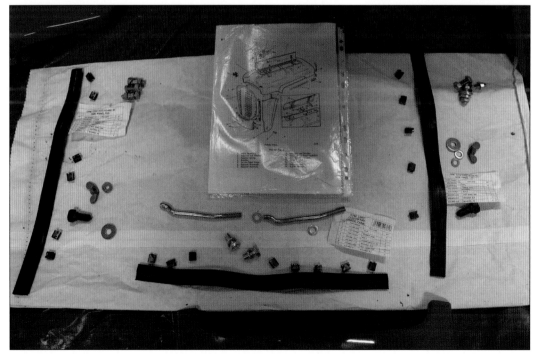

13.52. Layout of bits and pieces

Bodywork

13.53. This is the finished tractor.

About the Author

Chris Jaworski has 35 years of experience in agricultural engineering. He has been a technical author and further education lecturer at Bicton College, Devon. His students' tractor rebuilds for charity were a major feature of tractor shows in the UK and raised over £200,000 for Bicton Overseas Agricultural Trust. Chris has contributed articles to *Tractor & Machinery* magazine. *The Massey Ferguson 35 Tractor Workshop Service Manual* is his first book.

Replacement parts featured in this manual were supplied by: **VAP VAPORMATIC**

For details of other titles published by Old Pond,
please visit our website:

http://www.oldpond.com